SWAG IS NOT ENOUGH

CAREER ADVICE FOR THE SERIOUS MILLENNIAL

ALANA D. WYCHE
AND
KEITH R. WYCHE

authorHOUSE®

AuthorHouse™
1663 Liberty Drive
Bloomington, IN 47403
www.authorhouse.com
Phone: 1 (800) 839-8640

© 2016 Alana D. Wyche; Keith R. Wyche. All rights reserved.

No part of this book may be reproduced, stored in a retrieval system, or transmitted by any means without the written permission of the author.

This book is a work of non-fiction. Unless otherwise noted, the author and the publisher make no explicit guarantees as to the accuracy of the information contained in this book and in some cases, names of people and places have been altered to protect their privacy.

Published by AuthorHouse 01/07/2016

ISBN: 978-1-5049-6412-8 (sc)
ISBN: 978-1-5049-6413-5 (hc)
ISBN: 978-1-5049-6411-1 (e)

Library of Congress Control Number: 2015919741

Print information available on the last page.

Any people depicted in stock imagery provided by Thinkstock are models, and such images are being used for illustrative purposes only.
Certain stock imagery © Thinkstock.

This book is printed on acid-free paper.

Because of the dynamic nature of the Internet, any web addresses or links contained in this book may have changed since publication and may no longer be valid. The views expressed in this work are solely those of the author and do not necessarily reflect the views of the publisher, and the publisher hereby disclaims any responsibility for them.

I dedicate this book to my heroes (my parents), Keith and Denise.

CONTENTS

Chapter 1: CEO of Me, Inc. 1
  Managing Your Career Like an MVP 1
  We Are Witnesses 3
  Lead Your Value: Claim Your Throne of Success
      Before You Rock the Crown 4
  Lead Your Value: You Must Make "Me Me Me" Decisions 9
  Lead Your Network: Align Yourself with Agents of Change 14
  Five Qualities of Agents of Change 15
  The Baby Boomer's Reaction: Who Are These Kids? 17
  Advice to Millennials 19
  Advice to Boomers 19
Chapter 2: Brand It Like Beyoncé 20
  Realities of Making Your Professional Brand Marketable 20
  Welcome to the Beyoncé Experience 22
  So What's Your Brand DNA? 23
  Performance: Deliver Results; Drive Innovation! 25
  Performance Is Power 26
  How to Tap into Your Inner Intrapreneur 27
  Exposure: Find Someone to Help #UpgradeU 29

    Who's Wearing Your T-shirt? 29
    Mentors and Sponsors: You Must Have Them 30
    How to Find a Mentor 31
    Perception: Leave a Lasting Impression That Says "I Was Here" 33
    Do You Know How Others See You? 35
    How to Minimize Perception Gaps 36
    The Baby Boomer's Reaction: "Your Brand Can Make or
        Break You" 36
    Advice to Millennials 36
    Advice to Boomers 37
Chapter 3:   Safeguarding a Scandal-Free Image 38
    Because Olivia Pope Can't Save You 38
    Five Reasons Some Millennials Go Rogue 43
    Five Ways to Stay on P.O.I.N.T. 45
    Performance Boundary Principle: Showing Up Is Not Enough 46
    Online Boundary Principle: Keep Your Private
        Persona Invisible Online 48
    Individual Boundary Principle: Know Your Limits 49
    No-Go Boundary Principle: Don't Break the Career
        Commandments 51
    Taking Accountability Boundary Principle: The Right Way
        to Repair a Ruined Reputation 52
    The Baby Boomer's Reaction: Image, What Others
        Think of You Matters 53
    Advice to Millennials 53
    Advice to Boomers 54
Chapter 4:   Good Is Still Not Enough 55
    Don't Let Complacency Kill Your Career 55
    How the Comfort Zone of Complacency Becomes Dangerous 57
    Detouring from the Danger Zone of Mediocrity 59
    When In Doubt, Just W.O.W. 62
    Purpose-Identifying Questions 62
    The Baby Boomer's Reaction: Your A-game,
        Never Leave Home without It! 65
    Advice to Millennials 66
    Advice to Boomers 66

Chapter 5: Don't Get Caught in the Catfish Culture 67
   Social Media Does Not Replace Social Interaction 67
   Millennials Interrupted 68
   Rise of the Corporate Catfish Culture 70
   You Can't Filter a Poor Personality 70
   How to Sharpen Your Soft Skills 71
   The Baby Boomer's Reaction: I Thought Catfish
      Was Something You Eat 75
   Advice to Millennials 76
   Advice to Boomers 76
Chapter 6: So You Want to Be a Boss 77
   Learn How to Be a Leader First 77
   Old School Career Advancement 78
   Case Study: Career Advancement in the Millennial World 79
   Work Habits That Work in Your Career Advancement Favor 83
   More Rules for Connecting Like a Rock Star 87
   The Baby Boomer's Reaction: It's Not Your Father's Workplace 88
   Advice to Millennials 89
   Advice to Boomers 89
Chapter 7: Stir Up Start-up Success 90
   Tips for Turning Your Passion into Profits 90
   Top Factors Fueling Aspiring Millennial Moguls 92
   Common Mistakes That Sabotage Our Start-up Success 93
   Boss Moves Tips from Dana Brownlee 96
   A Millennial Mogul Making It Happen 97
   The Baby Boomer's Reaction: Do Your Thing! 100
   Advice to Millennials 100
   Advice to Boomers 100
Chapter 8: If I Knew Then What I Know Now 101
   A Conversation with My Twentysomething Self 101
   Enjoy the Journey 104

ACKNOWLEDGMENTS

First and above anyone else, I want to thank God for giving me the opportunity to achieve one of my life-long dreams. Next, I want to thank my father for being such an amazing visionary and allowing me to join him on his journey to empower others. Dad, you are by far my greatest mentor; and I appreciate all of the wisdom and love you've sown in my life.

To my mother, thank you for being a champion of your children. Mommy, thank you for always reminding me whose child I am. Your unwavering love, support, and "pushing" has helped me realize that yes, I can do all things through Christ who strengthens me. To my second mom and dad, Carla and Floyd, I love you both more than words can express. I am truly grateful to have you in my life. I wouldn't be the woman I am today, if not for having you as two of my biggest cheerleaders.

To my siblings, Ang, Kev, and Kyle, I love you dearly and I'm so proud of you all! Thanks for always having my back and holding me down! To my awesome family (far too many names to list), please know that I love, love, love you with all of my heart and appreciate you for always celebrating me. To my inner circle, Natasha, Kali, Dawn, Ashley, Adrienna, DeShawn, Kim, Cherisse, Kelsey, and Damian, thanks for being my closest friends and confidants. You inspire me so much!

Lastly, to all of my brilliant mentors, thank you for influencing my career: Audrey, Phyllis, Michelle, Pernether, Angie, Xavier, Andrew, Sonia, Caroline, Shannon, Chandra, Jessica, Robin, Darryl, Karen, Valerie, John, Genevieve, Monique, LaShana, LaToya, Imaeyen, Alfred, Kristen, Kirsten, Kimberly, Jodi, LaNee, Lisa, and Martha.

INTRODUCTION

It seems like only yesterday you were playing with your Sony PlayStations, holding your Cabbage Patch dolls, and loading your profiles onto MySpace. Now you are educated, employed, and energetic working professionals looking to make a difference in the world. However, it appears, in some circles, you are not understood, often underestimated, and seldom fully utilized for the value you can provide.

Welcome to the world of being a millennial. You are part of the most talked about, written about, and yet least understood generation in modern history. You were able to program a VCR and television remote control before you could speak. You were taught using the latest technology, distance learning, and online classes. You embraced social media and networking when most of the adult world couldn't spell Google or Twitter. And yet you find yourself misunderstood at best and marginalized at worst.

However, in reality, millennials possess some of the most innovative and creative minds in the workplace. Unlike previous generations who adhered to militaristic hierarchies and the "me too" group thinks and chose to live to work, you have decided that organizational layers create unproductive barriers, group think stifles creativity, and living to work leads to burnout. In your world your job is an extension of who you are, your coworkers are a broadening of your social network, and you choose to work to live so you can enjoy all life has to offer.

But in reality you have a serious problem. Most of today's leaders are from another time and place. Your bosses are baby boomers or Gen Xers (baby boomer wannabes) and, in some cases, traditionalists (Grandma and Grandpa). They can't seem to understand why you act and think how you do. They struggle to see you as equals in decision-making, and your grasp of technology can intimidate them. But until you are running the organization, you must learn how to work with, through, and beside them.

This book serves to enhance your ability to succeed by exploring common myths and perceptions regarding millennials. You will see yourselves through the eyes of others to better understand and ultimately overcome these misperceptions. Additionally it will force you to look at yourself in the mirror to uncover some of your blind spots and opportunities for personal and professional growth.

A millennial with editorial insights by her baby boomer father wrote *Swag Is Not Enough* and hopes, after reading, you will be armed with insights and lessons to take your career to new heights.

The true lesson, however, lies in the ability of humankind to truly embrace and recognize the power of diversity of thought and to recognize that everyone, by virtue of his or her unique backgrounds and experiences, brings a valuable and unique perspective to the organization. Perspectives, if they are embraced, can help drive innovation, productivity, and, ultimately, profit.

Finally we are to accept that embracing diversity is not enough. To truly harness its potential, diversity needs to be coupled with inclusion and equality. Diversity only invites you to the party. Inclusion gives you a seat at the table; equality provides you with the same opportunities for success that are provided to others. Without inclusion and equality, you will come to the party hungry and leave the festivities unsatisfied.

Chapter 1

CEO of Me, Inc.

Managing Your Career Like an MVP

As counterintuitive as it might seem, there is no better time for millennials to begin to plan and navigate their careers than the present. While undoubtedly our career journey will have many twists, turns, starts, and stops, embarking on such a journey without planning is akin to taking a long road trip without a map or at least an intended destination. The old saying says, "If you don't know where you're going, any road will lead you there."

But unlike our Gen X and baby boomer parents and grandparents, we aren't beholden to a prescribed career plan, industry, company, or even discipline. While our elders focused more on the destination, we millennials want to make sure we enjoy the journey. It's not all about the title, salary, or position on the organization chart. Job fulfillment for our generation comes from being actively engaged in helping shape the vision; having a voice in day-to-day decision-making; receiving acknowledgement for our contribution; and enjoying our work, our coworkers, and ourselves.

For millennials it's not enough to have a seat at the table; we also want a voice or say in what the meal will be. And unlike children assigned to the kiddie table at Thanksgiving, we want to be seen and heard. And a great example from our generation of someone who was determined to chart his own course began his journey from an unlikely place.

It was all a dream that dribbled to life on a linoleum floor on Macon Street at a Salvation Army in Akron, Ohio.[1] An eleven-year-old who idolized the Dream Team of Magic, Michael, and Larry was laying up shots to one day stand out as a king among titans. As he transformed into a teenager, he simultaneously morphed into the mega star he had dreamed about as a kid driving the ball to the basket game after game. He had the body of an NBA forward, the passing ability of a point guard, and wonderful jumping ability. He was featured on the cover of *Sports Illustrated*. He graced the front of *ESPN: The Magazine*. Two shoe companies were willing to give him millions of dollars for his services; basketballs with his autograph were selling on eBay for as much as four hundred dollars.[2] He led St. Vincent-St. Mary to three state championships in four seasons. He was named Ohio's Mr. Basketball for three straight seasons and named to *USA Today*'s All-USA First Team for three straight seasons. He finished his four-year high school career with totals of 2,657 points, 892 rebounds, and 523 assists.[3] By the time the phenom graduated with his high school diploma in hand, the inevitable was made official when the Cavaliers selected him with the first pick in the 2003 NBA Draft.

---

[1] *More Than a Game*, directed by Kristopher Belman (2008; Santa Monica, Calif.: Lionsgate, 2010), DVD.

[2] Mike White, "LeBron's the Name, High School Basketball is the Phenom's Game," *Post Gazette*, December 15, 2002, http://old.post-gazette.com/highschoolsports/20021215jamesp1.asp.

[3] Plain Dealer Sports, "Cleveland Cavaliers Choose LeBron James with No.1 Pick in 2003: Draft Rewind," *Cleveland Plain Dealer*, June 27, 2013, http://www.cleveland.com/cavs/index.ssf/2013/06/cleveland_cavaliers_choose_leb.html.

The rest is history. Today LeBron James, crowned the king of the court, is considered the greatest player in the league.[4]

We Are Witnesses

In November 2005, Nike erected a 110-foot-high by 212-foot-wide billboard adjacent to the Quickens Loan Arena, the home of the Cleveland Cavaliers. The gaudy advertisement featured an airborne LeBron James propelling his strikingly muscular figure toward the words "We are all witnesses."

He had not yet claimed an MVP award, won an NBA championship, or even appeared in the NBA Finals. While his dominant play in high school had transformed the way media covered that level of basketball, he had not yet become the transcendent, transgenerational, transcontinental mega star that had to be witnessed.

Consequently, the We Are All Witnesses campaign appeared somewhat preemptively. But Nike, like LeBron sailing above the rim, rarely misses. They knew what LeBron James would become. And they knew that positing spectators as witnesses was the best way to chart it. Nike knew that a witness is not just a fan. They understood that a witness has certain, very tangible responsibilities. A witness judges, moderates, and facilitates an athlete's ascension to greatness. A witness justifies the very object it observes. In its infinite marketing wisdom, Nike recognized that witnesses become actively invested in the fortunes of their subjects. They don't merely watch, dispassionate and distant; they witness, entrenched and involved.[5]

So how will you make the world a witness to your greatness? I believe, if we take a closer look at his story, we can find an answer in these leadership lessons:

- Lead Your Vision: Claim Your Throne of Success Before You Rock the Crown
- Lead Your Value: You Must Make "Me Me Me" Decisions

---

[4] Ibid.

[5] "We Are Witness," Dan's Sports Blog, January 1, 2014, http://dansportsblog.wordpress.com/2014/01/22/we-are-witness.

- Lead Your Network: Align Yourself with Agents of Change
- Lead Your Vision: Claim Your Throne of Success Before You Rock the Crown

Lead Your Value: Claim Your Throne of Success Before You Rock the Crown

A sixteen-year-old LeBron James once said, "They say I'm the best player in the country and I want to keep it that way."[6]

Long before he formally assumed the role of his royal NBA status, the four-time MVP winner believed in his own hype from day one. Throughout his career, the King of the Cavs practiced a very powerful success strategy that dates back to biblical days. He was a visionary of his own destiny.

According to Jack Canfield, creator of the *Chicken Soup for the Soul* series, the daily exercise of visualizing your dreams as already complete can rapidly accelerate your achievement of those dreams, goals, and ambitions. Visualization of your goals and desires accomplishes four very important things:

1. It activates your creative subconscious, which will start generating creative ideas to achieve your goal.
2. It programs your brain to more readily perceive and recognize the resources you will need to achieve your dreams.
3. It activates the law of attraction, thereby drawing into your life the people, resources, and circumstances you will need to achieve your goals.
4. It builds your internal motivation to take the necessary actions to achieve your dreams.[7]

---

[6] "16 Year Old Lebron James! (Pre-Jr. Year News Segment)," YouTube video, 2:10, posted by "PFlaw317," February 15, 2010, http://youtube/29SDllawaw8.

[7] Jack Canfield, "Visualize and Affirm Your Desired Outcomes: A Step-By-Step Guide," JackCanfield.com, April 1, 2014, http://jackcanfield.com/visualize-and-affirm-your-desired-outcomes-a-step-by-step-guide.

Vision Planning Is a Ritual, Not a Resolution

New Year's Eve is a magical time of year for millions of baby boomers and millennials alike that believe this date bestows a special power to ignite resolutions into results. Studies show, while 40 percent of us are actually diligent with making these seasonal goals, only 8 percent see them bloom to fruition.[8] However, when we talk in terms of managing our careers like an MVP, the feel-good fallacy of New Year's Eve goal-setting doesn't have any place in purpose-driven vision planning.

Millennial performance coach and fellow LeBron fan Jullien "The Innerviewer" Gordon expounds on this idea in his blog, "How to Set Winning Goals like LeBron James: 9 Questions to Ask Yourself before You Make Your Next Move." Gordon says,

> For Lebron James, New Year's Day is not January 1st. It's the last day of the NBA season. For example, after losing to the Dallas Mavericks in Game 7 of the 2011 NBA Finals, he went into a dark place—a place where I believe he dug deep and set goals for the upcoming season using these 9 questions, which ultimately resulted in an MVP, his first NBA Championship, and Finals MVP.
>
> - **Experience: I ultimately want to experience what it is like to be ...** When we start with the experience we want to create first, it opens us up to a variety of different goals we can set to gain that experience. For instance, if I want to experience financial freedom, several different goals or approaches may get me there, such as paying off my credit card debt, starting my side hustle after work, buying an income property, learning how to day-trade, reducing my cost of living, or increasing my income.
> - **Intention: Why is having this experience so important to me beyond just doing it?** The moment we declare what we want to be and experience, we tend to jump straight into doing an action. But before we do anything, it is important to establish

---

[8] Dan Diamond, "Just 8% of People Achieve Their New Year's Resolutions. Here's How They Do It," *Forbes*, January 1, 2013, http://www.forbes.com/sites/dandiamond/2013/01/01/just-8-of-people-achieve-their-new-years-resolutions-heres-how-they-did-it.

our why. Why is having this experience so important to us? Viktor Frankl once said, "A man who knows his why can bear almost any how."[9] Sometimes it's not that we don't know how to do something. Sometimes our why isn't big enough, and our inaction shows us that.

- **Growth: What limiting beliefs or feelings will be pushed by this experience?** Goals should require you to grow into someone you haven't been before. An activity that doesn't require growth is merely a to-do list item. If you accomplished all of your goals last year, you likely underestimated your abilities and didn't challenge yourself. If you didn't accomplish them all, you may have overestimated your abilities. This is where a thirty-day do-it list can provide great opportunities. They challenge the following chatter in our heads: "That I can't …", "That I'm too …", and "That people won't …" A great example of a thirty-day do-it list would be running a marathon in a certain time when you've only run half-marathons until now. Another example would be achieving sales of twenty thousand dollars in a week when your personal best is currently at fifteen thousand. A thirty-day do-it list should stretch you in a way that creates some uncertainty but also inspires you. This should challenge your limiting beliefs and expand your self-concept.
- *Gaps: What challenges or excuses do I see/foresee stopping me from creating this experience?* Before we even set new goals, many of us have our excuses ready in the back of our minds. Instead of dealing with our excuses after trying to achieve our goals, why not just deal with them all up front? Let's say, "Excuse me, excuses. I'm going to get you out the way now because having this experience is important to me and nothing is going to stop me." Imagine yourself thirty days into the future. Envision that you failed miserably at the goal you set. What would be all of the reasons you didn't do what you said you wanted to do? We know all of the common ones: I don't have time, I have the kids, I didn't have the money, I was too tired, Work got busy, My boss said/did this and that, My wife said/did this and that, and

---

[9] Viktor Frankl, *Man's Search for Meaning* (Boston: Beacon Press, 1968).

I didn't have any support. One of my favorite quotes is "Excuses are monuments of nothingness. They build bridges to nowhere. Those who use these tools of incompetence, seldom become anything but nothing at all."[10]

- **Support: How can I attempt to close these gaps in advance? Who or what can help me successfully create this experience?** Anytime we feel stuck or reach a plateau in our life, it's usually because we have exhausted our know-how. In those moments we end up doing more of the same, we hustle harder instead of smarter. When you don't know how to break through to a new level, one of the easiest things you can do is look for a course on coaching or consulting. A course will give you new information and insights. This will allow you to look at your situation with a new lens. Coaching will give you accountability and another perspective. Perhaps you have a blind spot or you're procrastinating on doing that very thing that makes the difference you seek. And a consultant will do what he or she can to get you to who and where you want to be with as little energy and effort as possible from you.
- **Effort: What are the actions that I am 100 percent accountable for to create this experience?** When you set a goal, differentiate between the action and the outcome. You can only hold yourself 100 percent accountable to the action and effort required to complete the action. You may do the action with all of your effort and still not achieve your desired outcome. For instance, you can go to the gym every day for three months and still not lose the twenty pounds you desired if your workout plan were not right. This is where a coach, friend, mentor, professional, or colleague comes in. He or she helps improve your strategy. He or she can help you make sure that you are engaged in right action through feedback while you focus on right effort. The world and economy are evolving faster than ever, and sometimes what we want and desire doesn't come to us in the exact way or form we expected it to. So be open (that is, hold onto your plan loosely), but stand firm in your intention.

---

[10] Unknown author

- **Initiation: What is the first domino? What's the easiest action I can do right now that will set my experience in motion?** Dates don't hold you accountable; events that involve other people and deliverables do. If you're serious about accomplishing a goal, create an event that involves other people where you will share a deliverable. A deliverable can be a document you create, photos, a proposal, or a demonstration (e.g., you weighing yourself in front of your accountability partners). It serves as proof that you did what you said you were going to do. As human beings we have a weird psychology about us where we are more comfortable disappointing ourselves than we are other people. So use it to your advantage by getting other people involved and promising to show them the results of your effort. For you, it may mean sending invitations, paying a coach or trainer, buying your tickets, or giving a friend a hundred dollars if you don't do what you say. Do whatever works for you.
- **Measurement: How will I measure my success during the experience?** Focus on your input and the journey as much as the outcome and the destination. Your life is your vehicle to design, drive, and maintain. So you need a dashboard. Though a dashboard has no functional use in a car getting from point A to point B, it lets you know how well the vehicle is doing along the way by measuring how hard, hot, far, and full the car is. Without a dashboard you could overheat, run out of gas, or break the speed limit. I invite all of you to create a visual dashboard for yourselves. Rather than leaving your goals as words, make a one-pager with bar graphs, pie charts, or check boxes so you can visually see where you are along your journey this year. If you have a savings goal of twenty thousand dollars, put a big bar graph on the back of your bedroom door and color it in as your savings grow. If you're giving up smoking, pin a ten-dollar bill to a calendar for each day you don't smoke to symbolize what you would have spent on a pack and celebrate that you didn't. Make

it visual. Other examples of measurements include pounds lost, running time, dollars earned, and number of new clients.
- **Authenticity: Do I accept this goal as an authentic, intentional choice of my own?** Look within and answer yes or no. While things we've heard and seen may influence our goals, in order to be fully committed, we have to fully own the goal as our own. People close to you can make recommendations and give advice, but at the end of the day, you have to determine if this is the right goal for you. Before you begin, get a clear yes or no and then go. The X factor to success is knowing your why. The clearer you are on the reason why you are doing anything before you even begin, the more likely it is that you will succeed.[11]

Lead Your Value: You Must Make "Me Me Me" Decisions

In 2013 journalist Joel Stein wrote a controversial *Time* magazine cover story, "Millennials: The Me, Me, Me Generation." Millennials, he concluded from curated "cold, hard data," suffered from narcissistic personality disorders nearly three times the rate of baby boomers.[12]

According to the Mayo Clinic, narcissistic personality disorder is a mental disorder in which people have an inflated sense of their own importance and a deep need for admiration. Those with narcissistic personality disorder believe they're superior to others and have little regard for other people's feelings.[13]

No one was more guilty of this than LeBron James, who announced "the decision" in 2010 to take his talents to South Beach, leaving behind Cleveland, the city that catapulted him to fame, in favor of being number one.

---

[11] Jullien Gordon, "How to Set Winning Goals Like LeBron: 9 Questions to Ask Yourself Before You Make Your Next Move," accessed September 2, 2014, http://julliengordon.com/how-to-set-winning-goals-like-lebron-james.

[12] Joel Stein, "Millennials: The Me, Me, Me Generation," *Time*, May 20, 2013, http://www.fandm.edu/uploads/media_items/stein-2013-me-generation.original.pdf.

[13] Mayo Clinic Staff, "Narcisstic Personality Disorder: Definition," Mayo Clinic, accessed September 1, 2014, http://www.mayoclinic.org/diseases-conditions/narcissistic-personality-disorder/basics/definition/con-20025568.

> I feel like it's going to give me the best opportunity to win and to win for multiple years, and not only just to win in the regular season or just to win five games in a row or three games in a row, I want to be able to win championships. And I feel like I can compete down there.[14]

Robert Tew once said, "Respect yourself enough to walk away from anything that no longer serves you, grows you, or makes you happy."[15]

Beyond just merely moving on to a better opportunity, not only was LeBron James placing a value on not just his livelihood, he was placing a focus on his happiness, growth, and vision. For many other millennials, including myself, there will come a time when we will have to make tough decisions that will only appease you.

- **There's the decision to bankroll emergency funds like a baby boomer.** Emergencies are the surprise situations we're constantly cautioned to save for, the untimely events we never feel prepared enough for. Nobody knows this better than a baby boomer. They budget for what personal finance expert Suze Orman calls the "what ifs in life,"[16] like a boss. For millennials, this is one "me me me" decision we should prioritize as well. Orman says,

  > "If you're getting a salary, I'd tell you to live on 50% of that salary. So let's say you're taking home $2,000/month, you should live on as if you're only taking home $1,000 and make your life work on $1,000/month. Now you have a $1,000/month you can save. And you keep saving until you have at least eight months to one year of an emergency fund. That's why putting away your

---

[14] Henry Abott, "LeBron James' Decision: The Transcript," ESPN, July 8, 2010, http://espn.go.com/blog/truehoop/post/_/id/17853/lebron-james-decision-the-transcript.

[15] http://livelifehappy.com/life-quotes/respect-yourself

[16] Suze Orman, "Money Tips from Suze Orman," www.suzeorman.com/resource-center/suze-orman-money-tips-video-collection/what-ifs-of-life.

paper is a priority according to millennial money expert Alan Moore, founder of Serenity Financial Consulting.[17]

Of course Orman can't count our coins. We all have differing levels of responsibilities and resources. However, the reality that life happens whether we like it or not should be enough to start a rainy day fund to save ourselves a world of stress later.

- **There's the decision to cover your assets.** In every business there exists a proverbial bus and the messy employees who like to throw their colleagues under it. Sometimes they are loudmouthed troublemakers like the hyenas in *The Lion King*. Sometimes they are nosey nuisances like Quinn Perkins in *Scandal*. Other times they are cold as ice like Miranda Priestly in *The Devil Wears Prada*. Most times they pretend to play nice like Cady Heron in *Mean Girls*. If you're fortunate enough to have a boss who sees the bus coming and pulls you out the way, consider yourself lucky.[18] But even that's not surefire security to protect yourself from becoming a target. The only foolproof way to protect yourself from becoming their prey is to keep a cover-your-assets (CYA) file in your arsenal. So what goes in a CYA file? Facts and nothing but facts, which my dad always says you can't argue. For example:
    - **Attendance:** HR is not exempt from making mistakes. After all they are only human too. Keep track of when you arrive/leave the office, when your job requires you to travel, and when you take approved time off (personal, sick, and vacation days).
    - **Meeting Minutes:** Keep taped audio recordings and handwritten notes clearly summarizing who, what, when, where, and so forth.

---

[17] Suze Orman, "Plan for the What Ifs in Life: I Lost my Job and Can't Support Myself. What Should I Do?" accessed September 2, 2014, http://www.suzeorman.com/resource-center/suze-orman-money-tips-video-collection/what-ifs-of-life.

[18] Jeff Haden, "8 Qualities That Make a Great Boss Unforgettable," LinkedIn.com, August 26, 2014, https://www.linkedin.com/pulse/article/20140826123205-20017018-8-qualities-that-make-great-bosses-unforgettable.

- **Emails, Memos, and Tickets:** This is anytime you carry out or collaborate on a project and/or organize a history of all correspondence between parties involved.
- **Praise:** If your manager commends you on a project verbally, in an email, over a text, or through a handwritten note, document it.
- **Performance Reviews:** Some managers allow their staff to write their own reviews and sign off later. Others don't. Either way, you should always request a final copy of your signed performance review. Always.

• **There's the decision to fall and get back up.** You will fail, and you will fall once, twice, or maybe more in your career. Don't run from it because, when you do, you miss the learning and the growth that making mistakes produce. I think Michael Jordan puts it best, "I've missed more than 9000 shots in my career. I've lost almost 300 games. 26 times, I've been trusted to take the game winning shot and missed. I've failed over and over and over again in my life. And that is why I succeed."[19]

• **There's the decision to recharge your batteries.** Much like having to break up with someone you don't want to hurt, there is never a right time to request time off from your boss. After all many managers seem lost without us. That's a good and a bad thing. It's a good thing because you are doing a good job at doing your job; it's a bad thing because there is a disconnect along your team's communication channels if you are the only collaborator capable of getting things done. (We'll address that later.) Whether you need to schedule a stay-at-home vacation or a mental health day, do yourself a favor and find time to recharge your batteries, especially if your employer has contractually agreed to pay for you to do so. Here's why.
  - **Burnout is a high price to pay for employees and businesses.** It's easy to see an absent employee as a bad thing for business, but an employee who's never absent may actually be worse. Numerous studies have shown that never

---

[19] "Michael Jordan – 'Failure,'" YouTube video, 0:31, posted by "212GroupInc," February 16, 2012, www.youtube.com/watch?v=GuXZFQKKF7A.

taking time off can set off a wide range of issues from health problems to burnout. In *Success Under Stress,* author Sharon Melnick writes that 80 percent of workers feel stress on the job and 70 percent of health-care provider visits are due to stress-related conditions. Employee vacations have a precise ending; physical and mental health problems do not.[20]

- **People report feeling better and ready for work after some time off.** In an *ABC News* article, clinical psychologist Francine Lederer observes that "most people have better life perspective and are more motivated to achieve their goals after a vacation." Lederer calls the impact of breaks on mental health "profound."[21] Employees also report feeling more creative after they've disconnected from work.
- **Vacations help us manage stress now and in the future.** Whether or not we take full advantage of our vacation days (and statistics show that most of us don't), we can acknowledge that vacations are an important way for people to relax and recharge their batteries. But there's more to it than that. Psychologist Deborah Mulhern suggests that not taking time off can make it harder for our minds and bodies to relax now and from now on. Mulhern says, "The neural connections that produce feelings of calm and peacefulness become weaker, making it actually more difficult to shift into less-stressed modes."[22] With the amount of stress we carry, we must cultivate resiliency.
- **Vacations are best, but all breaks are important.** Studies have shown that the human mind does better working for short, intense periods of time and then taking a quick break. Continuous work can actually cause people to feel blocked and unable to find solutions or perform their jobs well. In an article for the *New York Times,* Schwartz explains, "During

---

[20] Sharon Melnick, PhD, *Success Under Stress* (Amacom, 2013).

[21] Patricia Quigley, "Vacations Help Job and Health," ABC News Online, August 13, 2011 http://abcnews.go.com/Technology/vacations-2011-time-off-improves-productivity-reducing-stress/story?id=14293331.

[22] Ibid.

the day we move from a state of alertness progressively into physiological fatigue approximately every 90 minutes. Our bodies regularly tell us to take a break, but we often override these signals."[23] If you truly can't take defined vacations, incorporate small breaks in your day. Go to lunch with a friend, or close your office door and take a few deep breaths. Or surf the Internet for ten minutes! A *Wall Street Journal* article discussed research that those taking a Web-surfing rest break were significantly more productive and effective at tasks and reported lower levels of mental exhaustion and boredom with higher levels of engagement.[24]

- **There's the decision to dream bigger.** If the first rule of vision planning is answering the question "I ultimately want to experience what it is like to be …" exit strategies help us dream bigger every time we meet or exceed our goals. By having an exit strategy, we are engaging new experiences, which expose us to fresh challenges, skills, opportunities, and networks to create increased visibility and value for our brands.

Lead Your Network: Align Yourself with Agents of Change

In the Brand It Like Beyoncé chapter, we cover the importance of having mentors (people who prepare us to get noticed) and sponsors (people with the power to get us noticed). The takeaway is simple. Mentors and sponsors help to upgrade our performance, exposure, and perception on our behalf within our companies and/or industries.

Similarly when we address the lesson of leading our network, we have to pause and reflect on the individuals we link our loyalty to. It's not easy to single out people who've pledged their allegiance to us because they may have played a significant supporting role in our success stories. The truth is that everyone who is running with us now may not be purposed to go the places our passion and vision take us.

Just as companies analyze and measure the value their employees contribute to their corporations, we too must audit the net worth of the

---

[23] Tony Schwartz, "Relax! You'll Be More Productive," *New York Times*, February 9, 2013.

[24] Rachel Emma Silverman, *Wall Street Journal*, September 22, 2011.

connections in our network—family, friends, business associates, love interests, and so forth. Really ask ourselves: Are they pushing us to our vision or pulling us away from our vision?

Touré Roberts said, "Actualizing greatness will cost you … The price is so high that many will opt out … But those who understand they were born for greatness … will experience a limitless and unfathomable existence."[25]

"Experiencing limitless and unfathomable existences" are part inside job and part aligning ourselves to agents of change. We see a brilliant illustration of this through the bond between LeBron James and his agent, Rich Paul. In the *New York Times* article, "An Agent of Change: LeBron James's Representative Completes His Own Journey," author Joe Drape describes how their partnership came to be.

> Paul and James first crossed paths in the Akron-Canton Airport as they were about to board a flight to Atlanta. As the story goes, Lebron's attraction to an NFL jersey worn by Paul led to an initial conversation and a chance meeting. Paul, who at the time was literally selling jersey's out of the trunk of his car, had no idea that his future was about to change, forever. "It was fate," Paul said. "I could have missed the plane. I could have taken an earlier flight. I could have not worn the jersey. I could have been having a bad day and not spoken to him."[26]

Five Qualities of Agents of Change

When we talk about aligning our vision and values to an agent of change, I believe we should look for five qualities, as seen in the Rich Paul/LeBron James story.

---

[25] Touré Roberts, *Purpose Awakening* (Faith Words, 2014).

[26] Joe Drape, "An Agent of Change: LeBron James' Representative Completes His Own Journey," *New York Times*, August 17, 2014, http://www.nytimes.com/2014/08/18/sports/basketball/lebron-jamess-return-to-cleveland-completes-a-journey-for-rich-paul-too.html?_r=0.

1. **They lead their own vision.** When Rich Paul was building his throwback jersey business, he counted professional athletes like Juwan Howard among his clients and was looking to open a store with Andy Hyman, the Atlanta businessman who supplied the jerseys. He had to know what he was selling, so he drove to the Pro Football Hall of Fame in Canton, Ohio, to learn about the greats who had come before his time. He lent the jerseys to friends to wear to the nightclubs, where they talked up his product and handed out his cards. LeBron James was often seen in vintage Joe Namaths or Magic Johnsons. Paul always had a pile with them as they traveled the American Athletic Union (AAU) circuit. The jerseys he was buying for $160 were flying out of his trunk for $300; soon he had $15,000 a week in revenue.

2. **Add value to yours.** When James was crowned King of the Cavaliers in 2003, he handed over a paycheck to Paul. It was Paul's first two weeks of a fifty thousand-dollar annual salary to do what neither of them knew exactly. "He told me that he really didn't have a job for me, but that he wanted me close and we'd figure it out," Paul said.[27] Paul worked to make himself useful any way he could. Before professional fashion stylists became a vital part of an NBA star's entourage, Paul handled those duties for James. He helped James rehearse for his Nike commercials, suggesting ways for him to be funnier.

3. **They're addicted to listening.** When he met the billionaire investor Warren Buffett, he paid attention when Buffett told him to trust his gut. From the music and film impresario David Geffen, he learned the power of organization and need to surround himself with the best talent available. "I was a sponge," Paul said. "I just tuned in whenever we had these meetings. LeBron had no obligation to me. I was not entitled to anything. I wanted to be valuable."[28]

4. **And learning.** When Paul told James that he wanted to become an agent, his agent specifically, he knew he needed more

---

[27] Ibid.

[28] Ibid.

exposure to the business. "He wanted to learn the ropes," James said. "I told him whenever you are ready, let me know."[29] So Paul went to work for James' agent Leon Rose, who had negotiated James' extension with the Cavs in 2006 and whose practice was bought by CAA the following year. No one was surprised that Paul was good at recruiting talent, bringing aboard NBA players like Michael Kidd-Gilchrist, Tristan Thompson, and Eric Bledsoe. In a bruising business long on paranoia and short on friends, Paul had earned a reputation as a smart, straight-shooting negotiator.

5. **Above all, they invest in building a bond founded on integrity and loyalty.** LeBron James' decision to return to Cleveland involved many factors on and off the basketball court. But at the heart of James' homecoming is a promise made twelve years ago between a teenage basketball phenom and a self-made businessman selling throwback jerseys out of the trunk of his car. In an interview in a suite overlooking the University of Akron's football field, James, twenty-nine, recalled those conversations with Paul long before either of them was on the sports radar, let alone at its center. "He used to listen to me and how I was going to get out of the inner city and make a difference, and I used to listen to him say how he was going to get out and make a difference," James said. "Those conversations turned to how we are going to do it, and then to, why not do it together?"[30]

The Baby Boomer's Reaction: Who Are These Kids?

I have to admit it. I don't really understand the millennial generation. As a baby boomer and father of four millennials, at times they seem like aliens from another planet. To their credit I find them very creative, innovative, and tech-savvy. As I see them march into the workplace, they have boatloads of confidence, a ton of entitlement, and a touch of

---

[29] Ibid.

[30] Ibid.

I-know-it-all. What I find most challenging, however, is their need for immediate gratification.

However, we must realize to a large degree that they are victims of their environment. They grew up with instant everything. Microwave ovens prepared their meals in an instant. The Internet put information at their fingertips. They have hundreds of channels to choose from on their super large, flat screen, high-definition television or calculator-sized smartphone, all with on-demand programming so they can watch what they want, when they want, and where they want!

I've personally seen this behavior drive corporate leaders nuts, particularly as it pertains to managing the career expectations of their millennial workforce. These young people don't really see the need to have years of consistent performance in order to receive a raise, promotion, or expanded responsibility. In their minds, once they've proven they can do it once, they've learned enough, and they're ready to move on.

In one case while I had oversight for call centers for a major credit card issuer, I had a young professional request to be promoted to manager after only six months on the job. In her mind, she worked faster than the others did on her team, she had better call-handling metrics than her peers, and she knew the software and technology better than her boss did. After explaining to her that being a manager required more than speed and tech smarts, she still struggled to understand why I was holding her back.

Rather than get frustrated, I decided to make this a teachable moment. I suggested that she shadow her manager one day. During this time she would have to listen to and solve the employee concerns and demands. In addition she would have to deal with irate customers who demanded they need to speak to a supervisor when their requests weren't handled to their satisfaction. After eight hours of this experience, she asked to return to her normal role the next day.

When I later asked how things went, she replied, "I didn't realize that, as a manager, I would have to deal with all this people drama!"

Advice to Millennials

- You are wise to want to take control of your career. Too often people in my generation left that up to others. However, as you plan your career, give yourself the freedom and flexibility to learn from each experience. Take the time required to master the skill and demonstrate consistent performance.
- You may not need to spend years in a role before you are ready for more responsibility, but make no mistake about it. Experience matters. If you were about to undergo major surgery, would you want this to be your surgeon's first or second time performing this procedure?
- Older workers most likely won't have your technical savvy, but they can offer value. They've seen a tremendous amount of change, and they've learned a great deal. Make a point of listening and learning from them.

Advice to Boomers

- The reality is that millennials are here to stay. What's more, a new crop of them is entering the workforce. You can't ignore them. You need to make an effort to understand them, and you must embrace them.
- Since we know that experience is the best teacher, provide them with opportunities that will allow them to experience what they think they know. Every new swimmer thinks he or she is the next Michael Phelps until he or she dives into the deep end of the pool.
- Recognize that they will most likely move between roles and companies more so than you did. While you have them, harness their energy and enthusiasm and leverage their creativity and ingenuity to drive innovation.

Chapter 2

Brand It Like Beyoncé

Realities of Making Your Professional Brand Marketable

In *Time* magazine, Baz Luhrmann said, "She's gone beyond being a popular singer, even beyond being a pop-cultural icon … Right now, she is the heir apparent diva of the USA—the reigning national voice."[31]

At the close of 2013, Beyoncé pulled one the biggest power moves the music industry has ever seen. Just as the clock struck midnight on December 13, the mega pop star released her fifth self-titled album, *Beyoncé*, exclusively on iTunes with no warning, no promotion, no launch parties, and no advance play, a risk that record producer Teddy Riley sums up as pure genius. "She showed how only a true star can

---

[31] Baz Luhrmann, "The 2013 Time 100: Beyoncé," *Time*, April 18, 2013, http://time100.time.com/2013/04/18/time-100/slide/beyonce.

break this industry glass ceiling. When it comes to business savvy, she just joined the lists of the greats."[32]

The result was a smash success. The digital album debuted number one on the Billboard 200 chart[33] and broke iTunes records, surpassing one million copies sold worldwide within six days.[34]

There's no question that the only reason she could pull off a stunt like this is because she's Beyoncé. However, if we take a deeper look, even us common folks can learn something from the pop visionary, as Public Relations Student Society of America (PRSSA)blogger Ashley Monaghan puts it, "The album's success does indicate that if you build yourself as a brand, your connections and followers will be interested in the work you produce."[35]

This philosophy is what I believe is the basis of the PEP model we will discuss in this chapter. PEP, an acronym for performance, exposure, and perception, infers that performance is key but exposure and perception unlock the door. What better way to break down this paradigm than by using the example of a millennial who has perfected it.

---

[32] Teddy Riley, "No Stunt: Beyoncé's Sneak Attack on the Music Industry Resets the Rules," CNN, December 24, 2013, http://www.cnn.com/2013/12/23/opinion/beyonce-teddy-riley-opinion.

[33] Keith Caulfield, "It's Official: Beyoncé Makes History with Fifth No. 1 Album," Billboard Blog, December 17, 2013, http://www.billboard.com/articles/news/5840086/its-official-beyonce-makes-history-with-fifth-no-1-album.

[34] "Beyoncé Album Sets iTunes Sales Record, tops Billboard Chart," Reuters, December 18, 2013, http://www.reuters.com/article/2013/12/18/us-beyonce-itunes-idUSBRE9BH1BL20131218.

[35] Ashley Monaghan, "Why Beyoncé's Secret Album Was the Best PR Move Ever (Under Her Circumstances)," PRSSA Louisiana State University Blog, January 27, 2014, http://prssalsu.com/2014/01/27/why-beyonces-secret-album-was-the-best-pr-move-ever-under-her-circumstances.

Welcome to the Beyoncé Experience

Beyoncé said, "I don't have anything to prove to anyone. I only have to follow my heart and concentrate on what I want to say to the world. I run my world."[36]

Just as her lyrics express, Queen Bey, as her fans know her, is a girl who runs the world, like literally. As half of the royal couple of culture,[37] Mrs. Carter holds the top spot on both the *Time* 100 Most Influential People in the World and the *Forbes* 100 Most Powerful and Influential Musicians in the World lists. With an estimated net worth of three hundred million dollars, her handprint can be felt from fashion, food, film, music, politics, and philanthropy.

Since the age of eighteen, she has appeared as the face of powerhouse brands, including American Express, Nintendo DS, L'Oreal, Pepsi,[38] and H&M.[39] She's sold more than 118 million records globally, won 17 Grammy Awards, and earned the status of being the highest-paid African American musician of all time,[40] thanks to her iconic international tour, "The Mrs. Carter Show," which grossed more than two hundred million dollars in 2013–2014. Her social media circle boasts nearly sixty-five million Facebook fans, sixteen million Instagram followers, and fourteen million Twitter followers. If that weren't enough, she will even be the subject of a course at Rutgers University called "Politicizing Beyonce,"[41] proving she's more than an artist. She's a bona fide, bankable brand.

---

[36] Beyoncé Knowles R&B Queen, posted October 14, 2012, www.facebook.com/Beyonce.Knowles.RB.Queen.

[37] Baz Luhrmann, "The 2013 Time 100: Beyoncé," *Time*, April 18, 2013, http://time100.time.com/2013/04/18/time-100/slide/beyonce.

[38] Sammy Said, "The Most Expensive Celebrity Endorsements," The Richest Blog, October 5, 2013, http://www.therichest.com/luxury/most-expensive/the-most-expensive-celebrity-endorsements.

[39] Frank Hagler, "Time Most Influential 2013: Jay-Z and Beyoncé Make the Cut," PolicyMic Blog, April 23, 2013, http://www.policymic.com/articles/37161/time-most-influential-people-2013-jay-z-and-beyonce-make-the-cut.

[40] Brande Victorian, "Beyoncé to Be Highest Paid Black Musician at the End of Mrs. Carter Tour," February 20, 2014, http://madamenoire.com/402663/beyonce-highest-paid-black-musician-time-end-mrs-carter-tour.

[41] Ibid.

So What's Your Brand DNA?

One of the first things that a serious millennial professional must realize is that you are your brand. Furthermore, you already have a brand, whether you realize it or not. Based upon your attitude, work ethic, disposition, and other attributes, people know what to expect—or not—the minute you walk into a room.

So the question isn't if you have a brand; rather what is your brand? Are you a team player, willing to work collaboratively to solve problems? Or are you a lone wolf who struggles to partner well with others or has difficulty embracing concepts and ideas that are not your own? Is your brand one of innovation and creativity, or a "me too" status quo, that is, "I want to be like everyone else" brand?

As consumers we understand the concept of brand all too well. It's why we pay five dollars for a cup of our favorite coffee, two hundred dollars for our favorite jeans, and way too much for our favorite pair of shoes, both ladies and men. And it's not just the price that determines why we choose a certain brand; rather it's the quality and craftsmanship of the product, the way it makes us look and feel, and the perceived value it adds to our life.

This concept really becomes understandable when we look at automobiles. If asked, "What car is known as the Ultimate Driving Machine?" invariably the BMW brand comes to mind. When we think of the brand of vehicle known for safety, most car enthusiasts will mention the Volvo brand.

Likewise, if you ask your parents or grandparents about the 1980s automobile called the Yugo, you'll most likely hear that its brand represented less than acceptable quality. In fact auto critics laughed at the Yugo and branded it more of a toy than a car. They also pointed out a series of flaws, and as it happens, many were valid. Many owners complained of mechanical problems, including premature engine failure, bad brakes, poor shifter and transmission, faulty electrical systems, and terrible dealer service. The insurance industry faulted the car's crash worthiness, which also didn't help matters. Essentially one of the many jokes made about it could sum up the brand. For example:

Why does the Yugo have a heated rear window?

To keep your hands warm while you're pushing it.

As millennials, we need to pay close attention to our personal brands. We first need to understand what our brand is currently, determine what we want our brand to be, and decide to be dedicated and dutiful in managing our brand. As young professionals, we never want to be the Yugos within the organization.

Your personal brand is also so important because, to succeed in any endeavor, profession, or vocation in life, your brand will need to stand out. In a world starving for innovation, creativity, and diversity of thought, to be successful you can't be a "me too" brand. It's important, like Beyoncé, to distinguish yourself from the others in your field. Not only in the way you show up, but also in your behavior and actions.

How you distinguish yourself from your peers, how that behavior is perceived, and how you actually manage that perception is critical to advancement.

P.E.P. MODEL

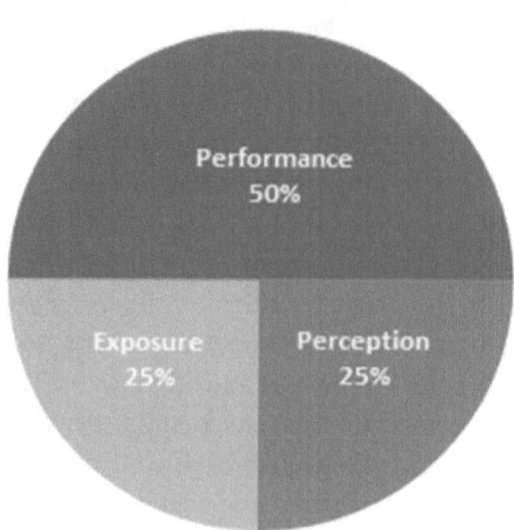

As we begin to explore the need and process of professional branding, we will cover three concepts: performance, exposure, and perception.

Performance: Deliver Results; Drive Innovation!

You have to be willing to put in the work! Of all the perceptions that exist about millennials, one of the most common is that they don't have a desire to put in the work. Perhaps this perception comes from the fact that technology expedited the way we receive and process information. Unlike my parents who attended college in the 1970s, my siblings and I could research in five minutes on the Internet what they would spend hours exploring in a library. So I would argue that it's not that millennials don't want to put in the work. Rather we choose to work smarter and faster, not longer and harder than necessary.

It is worth noting, however, that millennials must learn to appreciate the significance of experience and the importance of proper preparation if we are to be successful at the next level. Johnny "Johnny Football" Manziel, the Heisman trophy–winning quarterback from Texas A&M University, learned such a lesson the hard way during his first year in the National Football League. Playing for the Cleveland Browns, he was humbled by his poor performance during his initial season. Veteran NFL players, as he quickly learned, were much faster, stronger, and tougher than anything he experienced in college.

During the season he was ridiculed for partying late at night, being late for meetings, and even sending Twitter messages from his smartphone during an actual game. Asked to perform a self-evaluation at the end of the season, Manziel stated, "It's been a year of growing up for me. This is a job for me now and I have to take it a lot more seriously."[42]

The key lesson for Johnny Football and every other millennial is simple: at the end of the day, it's about how you perform once you get into the game. Furthermore, to perform well during the game requires the necessary preparation before the game.

Whenever my dad coaches young professionals on developing their assets, he challenges them to ask themselves the following questions:

1. What are your talents and gifts?
2. How have you used them in the past to achieve great things?
3. What is your personal greatest achievement?

---

[42] *The Cleveland Plain Dealer*, December 23, 2014.

4. How do you use your gifts to help others?
5. How do you want to be known? (What legacy do you want to leave?)

However, he states that the answer to his final question is the biggest determinant to the future success of the young professional. Namely, are you ready to put in the work?

Performance Is Power

Performance is a powerful tool for creating credibility for your brand. You want to be known as someone who not only works smart or hard but also delivers results. However, if you want to position yourself to advance to the next level, not only must you perform well against your peers, you must distinguish your performance by driving creativity and innovation.

According to millennial career expert, Dan Schawbel, author of *Promote Yourself: The New Rules for Career Success*, intrapreneurs—employees who function as entrepreneurs in a company[43]—is the new trend in generating awareness to your professional brand and subject matter expertise.

Schawbel chalks up intrapreneurship as the catalyst powering much of the product innovation visualized around the world today:

- At Lockheed Martin, intrapreneurs developed a number of famous aircraft designs.
- At 3M, they came up with Post-It Notes.
- At Google, they came up with Google News, AdSense, and Gmail.

Smart companies want you to become an intrapreneur because it fuels business growth and allows them to gain a competitive advantage in their industry. In a study conducted in partnership with American Express for his book, Schwabel found that 58 percent of managers are

---

[43] Phil Simon, "Millennials and the Workplace: An Interview with Dan Schawbel," Huffington Post, September 3, 2013, http://www.huffingtonpost.com/phil-simon/millennials-and-personal_b_3859114.html.

either very willing or extremely willing to support employees who want to capitalize on a new business opportunity within their company.[44]

How to Tap into Your Inner Intrapreneur

- **Build strategic alliances.** Think of your alliances as your own personal advocates. These people can help market you in ways you can't do alone. Your inner circle shouldn't be limited to your lunch crew or happy hour buddies. It should also include people who carry clout and presence within your organization. Branch out and make it your mission to foster meaningful relationships with people who will commit themselves to your success, proudly wearing your T-shirt before decision-makers in the boardroom and beyond.
- **Use social media to leverage your thought leadership.** Many people shy away from building an online presence in their fields because they don't feel they have anything to contribute or conclude that there isn't an audience who would find their work interesting. In most cases you won't know until you try. Internet stars spring up every day because they struck gold with one article, one video blog, or one picture that went viral. One such story is Mastin Kipp. During the height of the 2008 recession, Kipp, then twenty-eight and an unemployed record executive, started tweeting inspirational quotes to keep himself and friends encouraged. After a year of tweeting under the username @TheDailyLove, Kipp caught the attention of reality star Kim Kardashian, who then prompted her then two-million-plus followers to follow Kipp. With that single endorsement, @TheDailyLove grew from a thousand to ten thousand followers overnight.[45] Today, Kipp is close to hitting the six hundred thousand mark. The moral of the story is to not be afraid to beef up your digital brand. You never know who's watching or reading. Select platforms that make sense for your subject matter expertise

---

[44] Ibid.

[45] Mastin Kipp, "Contact," The Daily Love, accessed March 4, 2014, http://thedailylove.com/contact.

and target audience (e.g., Facebook, Google+, LinkedIn, Pinterest, Twitter, YouTube, and so forth). As a bonus, you can include these assets in a portfolio or presented in public speaking situations.

- **Participate in professional associations.** As the saying goes, membership has its privileges. Joining industry organizations add a great touch to your résumé. But don't just be a cardholder. Join a committee, roll up your sleeves, and flex your skills to help plan programs and push initiatives that will increase your brand awareness.
- **Get inside your boss' head.** Constructive feedback is a priceless resource your career development can't afford to live without. The very moment you begin reporting to your boss, make sure you have a clear understanding of what is required in your role by documenting the expectations your employer has established for you. Next, plan to meet with your manager at least quarterly. Be open to the having an honest and in-depth conversation about your progress and areas where you can improve. Conversely, as an intrapreneur, this is where you can especially shine by showcasing quantifiable examples of how your accomplishments have impacted the company's bottom line.
- **Attend formal and informal company events.** Love them or hate them, company events play a critical role in gaining exposure. These gatherings put you in spaces with direct access to executives and senior leaders who have decision-making power your next promotion or raise depends on. And if there is one rule you must always oblige, whenever you're extended an invitation, especially if it's to an exclusive informal event, you must RSVP and show your face. Several years ago I made the mistake of not attending an election day viewing party hosted by a company board member. It hadn't even been a year that I was on the job. I knew there were people who were more senior than I was who didn't get an invite, including some of my team members, and I felt awkward about going. So I respectfully declined and opted to attend an election day viewing party with my friends. Had I not been so concerned about what other people thought about me being at such an elite event, I would have rubbed elbows with key power players in a relaxed

setting that I would never have had the opportunity to do again. I am still kicking myself today over what I consider one of the worst decisions I ever made because I will never know what impact, if any, that would have made on my career with that company.

Exposure: Find Someone to Help #UpgradeU

A large part of why Beyoncé was able to achieve such phenomenal success early in her career was because she had someone willing to vouch for her long before the world knew she was a star. That someone was her first manager, her father.

During her 2009 "I am ... Yours" intimate concert at the Wynn Las Vegas, Beyoncé shared the story of how she got her foot in the door with her dad at the helm. As part of the girl group Destiny's Child, Beyoncé and the group's other members were less than ten years old when they set out on their dream. With her father, Matthew Knowles, as their manager, the girls were eager to land a record deal. However, fame and fortune eluded them for several years. While the girls could sing, they had maturity issues that could only be expected due to their age. A botched audition with a major label, a losing effort on *Star Search*, and even the pain of being signed and then dropped by Elektra Records didn't diminish her enthusiasm and drive.

> By the age of five I knew exactly what I wanted to be and that was a singer ... in 1995, we got signed to Columbia Records and in 1997 we were ready; and we came out with our first single "No, No, No."[46]

Who's Wearing Your T-shirt?

One of my father's favorite sayings is "No one climbs the ladder of success or breaks the glass ceiling on their own. Someone at the top of the ladder or someone who has already broken through the ceiling

---

[46] Beyoncé, "I Wanna Be Where You Are/Welcome to Hollywood," by Arthur Ross, Beyoncé, Leon Ware, R. Perry, S. Smith, and Shawn Carter, in *I am ... Yours: An Intimate Performance at Wynn Las Vegas Disc 02* (Sony Music Entertainment, 2009), CD.

has to see you, value what you bring, and pull you up and through." He then begins to describe a cartoon in which, in the first scenario, a couple is walking and holding hands. The man is wearing a T-shirt with the words "Damn, I'm Good." However, his companion has a look of displeasure and is frowning. In the second sequence, his female companion is wearing a T-shirt with the word's "Damn, He's Good" emblazoned on the front. The story suggests that you can't sing your own praises by wearing a T-shirt proclaiming your greatness, but your profile and credibility is enhanced when others wear your T-shirt.

In the business realm, it is essential that you have others wearing your T-shirt. You will need those who can speak to your competence, credibility, and ability to deliver when you aren't there to speak for yourself. From a career advancement standpoint, most organizations hold talent management or succession planning sessions annually where the business leaders, HR leaders, and others determine which individuals whose performance, results, and brand make them candidates for a promotion, a new assignment, or a special project. During these meetings, you need an advocate in the room wearing your T-shirt. As a millennial this can be an even greater challenge due to the stereotypes that some have regarding our abilities, expectations, and work ethic.

Mentors and Sponsors: You Must Have Them

Success is not a single act, and no one gets there alone. If you want achieve it, you will need the support of two critically important sources, mentors and sponsors. According to Bridget Van Kralingen, SVP of Global Business Services at IBM, mentors prepare people to move up, while sponsors make it happen.[47]

When she first joined Deloitte Consulting, she had just moved from her native South Africa to the United States. "A young partner in New York sat me down and said, 'Bridget, you have tremendous potential, but you're way too nice and polite.' That was great mentoring!" she says. "It helped me understand the cultural differences. I quickly adapted." She eventually became managing partner of Deloitte's financial services business.

---

[47] Anne Fisher, "Got a Mentor? Good. Now Find a Sponsor," *Fortune*, September 21, 2012, http://management.fortune.cnn.com/2012/09/21/women-mentorship-sponsorship.

At Big Blue, Van Kralingen recalls, "I had a sponsor who recommended me to run the financial services part of IBM's business consulting services in Europe and Africa—in spite of my lack of IBM experience. His advocacy both helped IBM to take a risk on me and helped me navigate the job."

As Van Kralingen's stories illustrate, mentors and sponsors teach, model, and encourage, helping you create a blueprint for your career, broaden your experience, recognize your strengths, and be emotionally prepared.

My very first mentor in the media industry was a veteran journalist named Sonia Alleyne. I was introduced to Sonia through my father after relocating to New York City upon graduating from the University of Toledo. At the time I was temping at a Manhattan law firm, making decent money but not living my passion.

When I met Sonia, her own story of breaking into journalism inspired me. A graduate of Emerson College, she got her start in the urban media space as an editor and credits the mentorship of another female editor with helping her navigate her way through the industry. Some of her notable highlights were serving as editor-in-chief of *Black Elegance*, a leading women's magazine; founding *Belle*, a publication for full-figured women; and interviewing the queen of media, Oprah Winfrey, for *Black Enterprise* magazine.

Being mentored by Sonia over the years has impacted my life immensely. She helped me get my foot in the door, and I've had many opportunities to learn and work closely with her. She planted many seeds of wisdom in my life, but one I carry with me to the power of authenticity. It's a fact that everyone may not like you or what you have to say. However, if you walk in your truth, passion, purpose, and faith, you will attract all the right people, opportunities, and blessings in your life.

How to Find a Mentor

Finding a mentor is a project, and in the words of life coach Iyanla Vanzant, you must be willing to do the work.[48] With patience and effort, the rewards can be life-changing. Kerry Hannon, author of *What's Next?*

---
[48] http://www.innervisionsworldwide.com/index.php?p=institute-workshops

Follow Your Passion and Find Your Dream Job, offers eleven tips to help you find a mentor or sponsor, no matter where you are in your career.

1. **Ask yourself what you want in a mentor or sponsor.** Is it an expert who can help with a specific business challenge—asking for a raise or finding ways to spiff up your image with the proper dress for success attire? Do you want someone inside your workplace who has the inside track to be an advocate for your project or promotion or someone who can act as a more general sounding board and big picture guide?
2. **Check your employer's HR department to see if they have a mentoring program.** Many big corporations—General Mills, Intel, Ernst & Young, Proctor & Gamble, American Express, Cisco, Citi, Deloitte, Intel, Morgan Stanley and Time Warner—offer sponsorship and mentoring programs. Entrepreneurs might tap into industry associations or SCORE.org, a nonprofit association and resource partner with the U.S. Small Business Administration (SBA).
3. **Look outside the office.** Mentoring doesn't have to be a business relationship. You can find mentors outside the workplace from associations you belong to, activities you're involved in, neighbors, and relatives.
4. **Do an Advanced People Search on LinkedIn.** You might search for someone from your alma mater. College ties do bind. You type in a title and your university, for example, current vice presidents of marketing and Duke University attendees. You can focus the search on your zip code or town so you can connect with someone nearby.
5. **Practice your "Why Me" speech.** This is a sales job. Landing a sponsor calls for self-promotion. You must toot your own horn, that is, your accomplishments, to get a higher-up's attention. They aren't going to back someone who doesn't have the potential to be a winner and make them look good. Skip the modest approach.
6. **Steer clear of the formal request.** The "Will you be my mentor?" invitation can be stiff and off-putting. It sounds like way too

much work and responsibility. This is an inner endeavor. Most mentors and sponsors primarily say they take the time to counsel and help because of the intangible satisfaction they get in paying it forward. Start by simply asking for advice on one action or problem.

7. **Show them how to help.** If you truly have a pressing need, take the plunge and make a specific request when you want someone to speak up on your behalf. Most people don't know where to start to help you.
8. **Make it fun.** When asking, don't make it sound like work. Exude a sense of excitement, smile, and laugh a little. Mentorship and sponsorship is an energy-boosting opportunity for both of you, and it often turns into a friendship. Find ways to meet regularly, even without an urgent agenda. Nurture the relationship.
9. **Do something for them.** Show your gratitude. Make the relationship reciprocal by serving as a source of information and support for your mentor in some way. It's the proverbial two-way street.
10. **Be a mentor.** This will give you a better idea of how to work with a mentor yourself. Even if you are at the bottom of your hierarchy at work, you might find mentees through alumni associations or nonprofits where you volunteer.
11. **Listen.** Whether you are the mentor or mentee, you can cultivate the relationship by asking questions and sincerely listening to the answers. Sometimes a mentor's most important input is to give practical feedback. Resist the knee-jerk urge to respond defensively.[49] Once your performance has received exposure, perception comes in to bring it all together.

Perception: Leave a Lasting Impression That Says "I Was Here"

Be aware of how others see you. In her song "I Was Here" on the album 4, Beyoncé sings, "I just want them to know, I gave my all, I did my best,

---

[49] Kerry Hannon, "How to Find a Mentor," *Forbes*, October 31, 2011, http://www.forbes.com/sites/kerryhannon/2011/10/31/how-to-find-a-mentor.

brought someone some happiness. Left this world a little better just because I was here."

In 2013 Beyoncé gave her fans and critics alike unprecedented access into her private life through the feature-length HBO documentary, *Beyoncé: Life Is But a Dream*. The film is a multifaceted portrait of her as a woman wearing many hats—singer, businesswoman, songwriter, actress, entrepreneur, wife, and mother—showing off the extraordinary gifts that have made her a global phenomenon and stripping away the veneer of stardom. It included extensive first-person footage, some of it shot by Beyoncé on her laptop, in which she reflects on the realities of celebrity, the refuge she finds onstage, and the transcendent joy of becoming a mother in 2012.

The film sheds light on her childhood in Houston with home movies revealing the close bond she built with her family and charts the challenges she felt when she decided to manage her career and build her own company, Parkwood Entertainment. The film also captures the intense physical and emotional demands she goes through in the studio, preparing for live performances, and running a business and her family life, including her return to the spotlight after the birth of her daughter, Blue Ivy Carter, in January 2012.[50]

According to Beyoncé, she decided to make the movie because she wanted to set the record straight about who she really was.

> I just wanted to cut through the noise. We live in a celebrity-obsessed culture where there's a lot of information traveling and a lot of talk, but if you really take a look you'll see that for the most part, it's not me doing the talking. Making a documentary was a chance to show who I am and what I really care about.[51]

That's what the perception piece is all about, managing how others shape their impressions of you. Where many people go wrong with this

---

[50] "Beyoncé: Life is But a Dream Documentary Special-About," HBO, accessed March 5, 2014, http://www.hbo.com/documentaries/beyonce/article/about.html#/documentaries/beyonce/article/about.html.

[51] Ibid.

is either not being self-aware from the gate or not caring how others see them at all.

Do You Know How Others See You?

As children we were raised to take the ridicule of others with a grain of salt. Many of our parents have recited variations of a famous quote from comedian W.C. Fields that says, "It ain't what they call you, it's what you answer to."[52] Although many of us wanted to embrace the notion that it's only what we thought of ourselves that counted, secretly we did care what others said, and it did shape us in some way.

Motivational blogger Lauren Messervey attributes that to the natural desire we possess as humans to be well-liked and well-received. From a very young age, we crave approval, but there is nothing more tragic in our early social lives than the discovery that we can't always be liked. From the moment we start talking and formulating our own ideas, the notion that some people will not like us confronts us.

Still more tragic is the fact that our words and opinions will be trapped in the consciousness of other people, turning us into hateful, odious people before we have even had the chance to show our true colors. Perception is king, and that king loves nothing more than to take control of everything around him.[53]

Every professional carries two perceptions: how you see yourself and how others see you. Controlling that perception as Beyoncé and Messervey suggests has to start and finish with making connections with people. People create ideas of you where they lack information. When you neglect to find ways to connect to people, you leave them no choice but to create an image in their minds of who they think you are. In the absence of information, people make up their own thoughts.

---

[52] Jack Canfield, *Chicken Soup for the Soul: Teens Talk Middle School* (Chicken Soup for the Soul, 2008), 42.

[53] Lauren Messervey, "Why Everyone Doesn't Like You," Huffington Post, March 4, 2014, http://www.huffingtonpost.ca/lauren-messervey/popularity_b_4880786.html.

How to Minimize Perception Gaps

- **Be personable.** The one quality that distinguishes you among all of your peers is your unique personality. Don't be afraid to let people see you are a real person. Being relatable makes it easier for people to communicate and trust you. Make sure you let people know who you are in the office and away from work as well.
- **Be known to everyone.** Communicate and connect with everyone on every level from the receptionist to the leader that sits at the top of the food chain. People don't care what you know until they know that you care. Display a willingness to help.
- **Be informed.** Become more self-aware and proactive with how you come off to others. Set aside time to sit down with people who know you very well to decipher if you are maintaining a strong, polished brand.

The Baby Boomer's Reaction: "Your Brand Can Make or Break You"

To have long-term success today in any field of endeavor requires that you are perceived as someone who delivers results and adds value. It is important that you are viewed as innovative, self-motivated, collaborative, and intellectually curious. Just as in building a house, the foundation you set for your personal brand today will either hinder or help you grow in your field tomorrow.

So while it important to maintain a healthy sense of self, it is equally as important to remember that you are your own brand. And as such, you need to manage, cultivate, and protect your brand at all cost.

Advice to Millennials

- Take time to understand what your current brand is. What do others see as your strengths and your weaknesses? Ask both those who work with you as well as friends and family to get a balanced perspective.

- For any perceived weaknesses, if you agree these are areas for development, put together a plan to address them. Perhaps further education, additional practice (e.g., if public speaking is a concern), or work with a mentor/coach to help you improve.
- If you receive negative feedback that you don't agree with, rather than getting defensive or upset, ask for examples of when you have demonstrated this behavior. If they can cite instances, it might open your eyes to a blind spot you might have. If they can't provide cases, kindly ask them to call you on this behavior the next time they observe it.
- Never forget that your brand will help you stand out (positively or negatively) in the workplace. Protect it!

Advice to Boomers

- The concept around personal branding is really one that you can help millennials to understand and embrace. At this point in their lives, they honestly don't know what they don't know. Share your lessons learned with them and knowledge on how you've had to build and perhaps even repair your brand over the years.
- Look for opportunities to mentor millennials in crafting their brand; encourage them to be continuous learners. Suggest articles and books that will broaden their perspectives.
- Provide shadowing opportunities to give millennials insight and exposure.
- Be sensitive to the fact that these young professionals grew up in a "show all-tell all" world. As such, they might not be aware of the dangers of social media and ways it can impact their brand.
- Be patient. Remember: you were young once!

Chapter 3

Safeguarding a Scandal-Free Image

Because Olivia Pope Can't Save You

On television, when Washington's wealthy and political elite need situations slain or sources silenced, they call on Olivia Pope to handle it. Pope, America's favorite fixer, fashionista, and side chick, is the central character on ABC's steamy drama *Scandal* starring Kerry Washington. She is a cleanup woman in every way, whose clout trumps even the highest the level of top-secret security clearance. With the slightest whisper of a single command, lies, liaisons, and loose ends disappear without a trace. Of course all of the sex, drugs, and deception make for great TV. In real life, where social media ruins more credibility than lying on your résumé, staying scandal-free isn't quite that simple.

In reality, at some point during your professional career, you are going to screw up. It might be a botched presentation, an inappropriate comment, or perhaps an ill-advised Instagram or Facebook post.

Furthermore millennials aren't the only ones who fall victim to scandalous behavior. From former congressmen like Anthony Weiner and Jesse Jackson Jr. to professional athletes, business and religious leaders, and entertainers, no one is immune. The challenge relative to managing your image and protecting your brand comes down to two things:

- avoiding catastrophic, career-ending mistakes
- rebuilding your image and brand after a fall

Let's take a look at three infamous cases of millennial misbehavior.

Kim Kardashian, Reality Star / Sex Tape Actress

Kim Kardashian said, "Your reputation is all that you have, and if people prejudge you over something that you did, than that kind of sticks with you a long time."[54]

Before breaking ground as the first reality TV star to grace the cover of Anna Wintour's fashion bible, *Vogue* magazine, Kim Kardashian was a celebrity stylist in the social circles of Hollywood starlets, including Paris Hilton, Lindsay Lohan,[55] and Nicole Richie. By 2003 she landed her first in a series of rumored high-profile love interests that included R&B singer Ray J (2003–2006), NFL running back Reggie Bush (2006), pop singer Nick Lachey (2006), media mogul Nick Cannon (2006–2007), rapper The Game (2007–2010), model Gabriel Aubry (2010), NFL wide receiver Miles Austin (2010), NBA power forward Kris Humphries (2011–2013), and rapper Kanye West (2012–present).[56]

In 2007, a year after she closed the chapter of her relationship with Ray J, Vivid Entertainment, a California-based adult film company, illegally acquired a sex tape starring the two lovers. Vivid, which paid

---

[54] "Kim Kardashian Biography," http://www.biography.com/people/kim-kardashian-450760.

[55] "Kim Kardashian Biography," *People*, accessed April 24, 2014, http://www.people.com/people/kim_kardashian/biography.

[56] "Kim Kardashian Relationship History," Who's Dated Who, accessed April 23, 2014, http://www.whosdatedwho.com/tpx_3339/kim-kardashian.

a million dollars for rights to the thirty-minute tape, widely promoted the release of the video, which it called *Kim Kardashian Superstar*. Kardashian quickly countered with legal action, suing for invasion of privacy. Shortly after the video's debut, she agreed to a five million-dollar settlement.[57]

Chris Brown, Grammy Award–Winning Artist / Bad Boy

Chris Brown said, "I feel remorse every day. I'm very ashamed. But it doesn't define me. I try to think about influencing people not to take the road I did."[58]

Just as Usher Raymond was preparing to press pause on his music career following the commercial success of his 2004 *Confessions* album, former Def Jam A&R Tina Davis was grooming a young Chris Brown to step in and steal his crown. His smooth voice, Michael Jackson–esque dance moves, and boy-next-door charm bolstered a deal with Jive Records, the powerhouse music label behind other show-stopping millennial acts such as Britney Spears and N'Sync.[59]

When Brown released his first single "Run It!," featuring Harlem rapper Julez Santana, there was no question who the new prince of R&B was. From 2005 to 2009, he was a seemingly unstoppable force in entertainment with a portfolio of platinum-selling albums, awards, and acting roles. While hearts all over the world lusted after the crooner, Brown found love with just one, sexy siren Rihanna. Shortly after the stars shared the stage at the 2007 MTV VMAs, delivering a sizzling hot performance of their hit songs "Wall to Wall" and "Umbrella,"[60] a torrid affair ignited and exploded.

---

[57] "Kim Kardashian," Biography.com, accessed April 23, 2014, http://www.biography.com/people/kim-kardashian-450760#synopsis&awesm=~oCjDcOST5uR8bv.

[58] Elizabeth Leonard, "Chris Brown 'I'm Very Ashamed'," *People*, September 14, 2009, http://www.people.com/people/archive/article/0,20306440,00.html.

[59] "Chris Brown," accessed April 24, 2014, http://www.biography.com/people/chris-brown-265946#awesm=~oCnppERnv6zBiM.

[60] Kara Warner, "Hottest Debut Performance Winner: Chris Brown and Rihanna's Electric 2007 Set," MTV, September 4, 2012, http://www.mtv.com/news/articles/1693095/chris-brown-rihanna-best-vma-debut.jhtml.

Similar to other storied celebrity romances (John Mayer and Katie Perry, Justin Bieber and Selena Gomez, Taylor Swift and all her exes, and so forth) their chemistry erupted into total chaos and countless troubles for Brown. The greatest of which still haunts him today. He assaulted Rihanna on their way home from a pre-Grammy Awards party on February 8, 2009.[61]

Justine Sacco, PR Hack / Social Media Outcast

Justine Sacco said, "Words cannot express how sorry I am, and how necessary it is for me to apologize to the people of South Africa, who I have offended due to a needless and careless tweet."[62]

Public relations seemed like the perfect fit for Justine Sacco. As the senior director of corporate communications for IAC/InterActiveCorp, Sacco spearheaded the media relations strategy of over 150 of the organization's media and digital properties, including the Daily Beast, About.com, and Match.com, to name a few.

A LinkedIn contact described her as "a great leader and manager. Her attention to detail, the multiple tasks she is able to handle and the pleasant interaction you have with her is truly amazing."[63]

Professionally she was an expert at preserving a polished professional image, but on the Internet, she was a social media deviant. Her self-described "troublemaker on the side"[64] alter ego produced some of the most repulsive off-color humor:

---

[61] Elizabeth Durand Streisand, "Chris Brown: A Timeline of Troubles," Yahoo Celebrity, March 14, 2014, https://celebrity.yahoo.com/blogs/yahoo-celebrity/chris-brown--a-timeline-of-troubles-165456789.html.

[62] Kami Dimitrova, Shahriar Rahmanzadeh, and Jane Lipman, "Justine Sacco, Fired after Tweet on AIDS in Africa, Issues Apology," ABC News, December 22, 2013, http://abcnews.go.com/International/justine-sacco-fired-tweet-aids-africa-issues-apology/story?id=21301833.

[63] "Justine Sacco Recommendation," LinkedIn Public Profile, accessed April 24, 2014, https://www.linakedin.com/profile/view?id=6292580&authType=NAME_SEARCH&authToken=gahF&locale=en_US&srchid=547727171398371847335&srchindex=&srchtotal=5&trk=vsrp_people_res_name&trkInfo=VSRPsearchId%3A547727171398371847335%2CVSRPtarget Id%3A6292580%2CVSRPcmpt%3Aprimary#recommendations.

[64] Chris Taylor, "Twitter Turns Ugly Over Idiotic Tweet," Mashable, December 20, 2013, http://mashable.com/2013/12/20/justine-sacco.

> As I sit and eat a bagel with lox, I would like to send love to my Jews who are all starving themselves right now. #hungryhungryhebrews
>
> — Justine Sacco (@JustineSacco) October 8, 2011
>
> Someone get the rape kit ready for Tom Brady. Go Giants! #SuperBowl
>
> — Justine Sacco (@JustineSacco) February 5, 2012
>
> I had a sex dream about an autistic kid last night. #fml
>
> — Justine Sacco (@JustineSacco) February 24, 2012
>
> In #NY, crazy men say "marry me gorgeous." In #London they say "you filthy cu_ts" cc: @kzarem@Leigh_Barratt
>
> — Justine Sacco (@JustineSacco) December 4, 2012
>
> "Weird German Dude: You're in first class. It's 2014. Get some deodorant." -Inner monologue as I inhale BO. Thank god for pharmaceuticals.
>
> — Justine Sacco (@JustineSacco) December 20, 2013[65]

But as the stillness of the 2013 holiday season approached, the jokester decided to shake up a slow news day and went a little too far. On Saturday, December 21, at 10:19 AM, minutes before boarding an eleven-hour international flight to her native South Africa, Sacco posted the following tweet to her two hundred[66] Twitter

---

[65] Jenvesp (*Buzzfeed* User), "16 Tweets Justine Sacco Regrets," Buzzfeed, December 20, 2013, http://www.buzzfeed.com/jenvesp/16-tweets-justine-sacco-regrets-hxg7.

[66] Allison Vingiano, "This Is How a Woman's Offensive Tweet Became the World's Top Story," Buzzfeed, December 21, 2013, http://www.buzzfeed.com/alisonvingiano/this-is-how-a-womans-offensive-tweet-became-the-worlds-top-s.

followers: *Going to Africa. Hope I don't get AIDS. Just kidding. I'm white!*

By 1:30 PM, an unnamed source had emailed the tweet to *Valleywag* blog editor Sam Biddle. Biddle did the only thing any connected millennial would have done. He wrote a blog and retweeted the link, setting social media on fire.

Just before 5:30 PM, the hashtag #HasJustineLanded was trending worldwide. Spoof twitter handles including @LolJustineSacco and @JustinePyscho started springing up. AID for Africa capitalized on the chaos by purchasing the domain www.justinesacco.com to promote AIDS fund-raising. At 11:30 PM, it appeared the news had caught up with Sacco, who deleted her Twitter account and tweet without offering an apology.

Media outlets, including the *New York Times*, CNN, ABC, BBC, and more, covered the Twitter storm. IAC issued a statement that they were "parting ways." Nearly twenty-four hours later, Sacco released an apology through a South African newspaper and then ABC News.[67]

Five Reasons Some Millennials Go Rogue

The question in the back of most people's mind is what causes an otherwise rationally thinking person to make such reputation-killing decisions like the stories illustrated above. In truth, bad mistakes happen to good people. If we were to look beyond that, we'd find that our lack of self-awareness trips us up. Let's look a deeper at what contributes to our consciousness struggle.

- **The millennial culture embodies the spirit of self-expression.** We are the rebel generation and can thank our parents in part for that. Yes, as youth, our parents encouraged us to be ourselves,

---

[67] Ibid.

lead and not follow, and, most importantly, not worry about what others thought about us. But they forgot to teach us how to tame that attitude as we became young adults, and we ran wild with their wisdom.

- **We have the innate desire for instant gratification.** Quick, fast, and in a hurry has been a way of life for many a millennial. As the second generation to witness the innovation of popular gadgets including the personal computer, video game system, DVD player, and cell phone[68], it's no surprise that we are the most tech-savvy generation of all time. In many ways, the luxury of technology has conditioned us to want what we want, how we want it, and when we want it. So some of us have become increasingly impatient and impulsive. Anxiousness has a way of breeding bad decision-making that gives birth to reputation-killing consequences.

- **Social media has magnified our problems.** Let's be real. Millennials did not invent the art of the scandal. Our forefathers mastered that for us. However, that doesn't stop our leaders from accusing us of demonstrating the most deplorable behavior of all time. Sure, we are considerably less conservative than baby boomers; however, I believe our flaws are grossly exaggerated because of technology. As the connected generation of the world, many of us live every waking moment of our lives on social media. So because we operate with an open book policy, our mistakes seem worse. Believe me, once upon a time, our parents were young too and not always as polished as they present themselves to be in their old age.

- **We have a self-ie obsession.** Crisis communications expert Judy Smith, the real-life inspiration behind Olivia Pope, has found that an "ego without limits" is the leading cause of character meltdowns. In her critically acclaimed book, *Good Self, Bad Self*, she asserts, "The balance that keeps someone with a healthy sense of self from becoming a self-involved egocentric person is tipped when the ambitions of self, run roughshod over the

---

[68] "Meet the Generations," Culture Coach International, accessed May 6, 2014, http://www.culturecoach.biz/Generations/meetthegenerations.html.

needs of others. Because when the ego rampages unchecked, it stomps on good judgment, self-analysis, and self-control. An ego without limits is like a car with no brakes; if you can't figure out how to regain control, you may wind up driving right off of a cliff."[69]

- **We take turning up too far.** Booze, business, and boundaries often collide at networking conferences and company-sponsored social events. From twerking on a CEO to toppling over from being sloppy drunk, I've heard and witnessed firsthand some of the most bizarre behavior in these informal settings. While you may strip yourself of being employee X after business hours, the truth is that you never turn off being professional. Our brands are a 24-7 mechanism that works even we're not on the clock. This is not to say that you can't have fun, but just use some good judgment because you don't want to face a messy morning-after experience.

Five Ways to Stay on P.O.I.N.T.

One of my all-time favorite sitcoms was *The Office*. Based on the award-winning BBC hit, the show was a parody of modern American corporate life that delved into the lives of the workers at Dunder Mifflin, a paper supply company in Scranton, Pennsylvania. This mockumentary NBC series[70] featured some of the most foolish antics and crazy characters similar to what many of us have seen in our very own work settings:

- Ineffective bosses whose leadership style is a total joke
- "Keep it 100" colleagues who make the most politically incorrect comments
- Title-hungry colleagues who can't be trusted
- Camouflage workers who collect a check for posing as a productive professional

---

[69] Judy Smith, *Good Self, Bad Self* (New York: Free Press, 2012), 19–20.

[70] "About the Show," *The Office*, accessed May 7, 2014, http://www.nbc.com/the-office/about.

- Sales staffers who sleep with clients or vendors for kickbacks
- Department comedians who bully coworkers
- Kissing coworkers who live their love affairs out loud in the office

While it's funny to see this recklessness play out on television, in the real world, these examples of distasteful conduct is no laughing matter. In fact, if you don't take your professionalism or perception seriously, your career will end up becoming a joke.

In this chapter, we are going to break down the five boundary principles you need to know to stay on P.O.I.N.T. and preserve a polished image:

- Performance Boundaries
- Online Boundaries
- Individual Boundaries
- No-Go Boundaries
- Taking Accountability

Performance Boundary Principle: Showing Up Is Not Enough

Mastering professionalism and performance comes down to more than just showing up and looking polished. It's understanding how to play your position and matching your assigned expectations with your best effort.

The best way to ensure you're keeping yourself in check is to have a solid C+D (communication and documentation) system in your career game. Amy DuBois Barnett, award-winning journalist and author of *Get Yours!*, provides insights into taking charge of your professional boundaries.

- **Be clear.** No matter what your field, communication is key, and perception is reality. You never want to be misunderstood. Express yourself well with the right tone, words, and volume for small meetings and in front of large groups. Join an organization

like Toastmasters to help you learn how to present yourself to the absolute best of your abilities.
- **Keep a record.** Every time you go above and beyond the call of duty, make sure to write it down. Your boss may or may not notice the extra project and hours you're working, but being clear about your accomplishments and being able to back them up with specific examples will be very helpful when you ask to be considered for new opportunities.
- **Manage upward and sideways.** You have a boss, sure, but in a way, you manage your relationship with him or her. Boss management entails respect, not blind obedience. Ask the right questions, and don't waste their time. Know your boundaries. You should develop and maintain a rapport with him or her so your conversations about new projects, promotions, raises, and so forth will go smoothly. You also want to manage your relationship with your peers. They will largely determine your reputation at your company. Do not make the mistake of ignoring their influence on your success. Be considerate, helpful, and fair. And don't succumb to office gossip or temptation to be mean or condescending. It will bite you in the butt eventually.
- **Refuse poor treatment.** Begin by telling the person who dares try to mistreat you that you will not tolerate it. If it continues, go through the proper channels to make sure you make your complaints by the book. Keep records of every instance of unfairness so you have evidence.
- **Don't let email run your day.** Those dings in your inbox can drive you to distraction. So turn off those message alerts and concentrate on the tasks at hand. Schedule specific times every day to read and return emails. (The frequency depends on the industry you're in.)
- **Do you still love it?** You may be the sort of person who finds his or her calling early or, like me, goes on a quest. Either way, you should evaluate your professional happiness regularly to see if you need to make a change.
- **Know when to quit.** Even an optimist like me knows that not everything is going to go your way. I have fought for jobs/

assignments/promotions and seen them go to someone else. I have tried to get people on my side who just wouldn't budge. And sometimes you just get bored and silly. Your gut will tell you when it's time to walk away and move your sights to the next opportunity.[71]

Online Boundary Principle: Keep Your Private Persona Invisible Online

As more companies use social media as a strong recruitment and retention tool, it's more important than ever to keep your digital presence in check. Let's start with debunking one of the biggest misconceptions about the Internet: your published profiles and posts are your personal business. Clearly as we've learned from the Justine Sacco saga, there is no privacy in a public domain. And what you don't know about your online reputation can hurt you.

According to Tory Johnson, founder of Women for Hire, "your digital identity—what's revealed about you in simple search results—can impact your career, your finances, and your personal and professional relationships. Fairly or unfairly, we often believe what we read online, which means we're all responsible for proactively managing our online persona."[72]

Ivana Taylor, publisher of DIY Marketers, takes it a step further and says it's totally possible to safeguard your online reputation.

1. **Set up Google Alerts for your name.** Head over to the Google alert page, www.google.com/alerts, and in less than ten minutes, you can establish a name alert. This way, you'll always be aware when something is being said about you online, positive or negative.

---

[71] Amy DuBois Barnett, *Get Yours!* (New York: Broadway Books, 2007), 116–117.

[72] LearnVest, "Is Online Reputation Really Worth the Money?" *Forbes*, July 26, 2013, http://www.forbes.com/sites/learnvest/2013/07/26/is-online-reputation-management-worth-the-money.

2. **Complete those social media profiles.** Many employees and business owners fail to do this. If you don't exist on LinkedIn and Twitter or, worse, your profiles are incomplete, it leaves the barn door open to trash your reputation. After all, if someone says something bad about you and people search social media and see nothing or something incomplete about you, whatever that person has written will carry more value.
3. **Create a flood of positive content.** Think of Google as your home page. When someone searches for your name or your company name, what he or she sees on Google will form an impression of you. So if you constantly create content that's credible, valuable, and reputable, a single negative post or comment will simply get lost.
4. **Present yourself as you'd prefer to be perceived.** People form impressions about you and your business by the way you appear online. Using a party picture on LinkedIn doesn't make a good impression, so take the time to have some professional-looking photos taken. This is a small investment up front, but it will pay off in the long term. Maintaining a squeaky-clean online presence should be high on your to-do list.[73]

Individual Boundary Principle: Know Your Limits

Perhaps the most complex workplace boundaries we have to consider are personal limitations because they are unique to each individual professional and ultimately impact how we manage other boundaries in business. Oftentimes the communities we grow up in, the values we're raised on, and the cultural experiences we are exposed to shape some of the biggest boundaries in business.

- **Behavioral boundaries:** What level of intimacy are you comfortable with? What about a boss who talks about his or her intimate details or asks you about personal concerns, finances, or your sex life? If you go along with it, even though you feel

---
[73] Ibid.

uncomfortable, this is your boundary weakness because you are not managing your borders. The best way to fix this is to create boundary awareness. Recognize your own periphery, and ignore the person or give feedback.

- **Physical boundaries:** This might be about touching or invading a person's space, for example, opening a person's drawer in his or her desk, searching through a bag, or even reading over someone's shoulder. All this can upset a person at work because another person is stepping over a boundary.
- **Ethical boundaries:** One of the challenges we see almost every day in business is some individual, group, or organizations behaving badly. It is essential that you adhere to your organization's code of conduct guidelines and operate from a solid moral compass. Integrity will take you a long way.
- **Mental boundaries:** Constructive conflict is a fact of life in relationships, business, and religious organizations. However, to be effective, you will need to display and assert your personal ideas, while at the same time being open to the ideas and thoughts of others. Being able to have mental boundaries allows you to stand firm and hold to your core beliefs and yet be flexible enough to accept others' ideas. This enables you to disagree with being disagreeable.
- **Emotional boundaries:** The reality is that we are human beings and, as such, our emotions can sway us. Left unchecked our emotions can cause us to be selfish, insecure, angry, and a host of other negative behaviors that can derail success. To be effective you must be in touch with your feelings, secure in who you are, and work tirelessly to manage your emotions. Those who are not effective at this can be branded a loose cannon, a bull in a china shop, or some other stereotype that limits your effectiveness. My dad, a former hothead in the boardroom, learned he had to learn to wed sound intellect with stable emotions in order to be successful.

No-Go Boundary Principle: Don't Break the Career Commandments

The other side of professional boundaries includes what we call "no-go behavior blunders." Sometimes we see them as innocent indiscretions; however, they are essentially unethical violations that can create catastrophic consequences and toxic work climates. Common examples of these crooked practices comprise deliberate deceptive or coercive[74] tactics including. Following are ten career commandments you must abide by.

1. Thou shall not abuse company credit cards with non-business-related expenses. Think before you swipe, and if you have to think about it too long, it's wrong.
2. Thou shall not backstab team members by taking credit for their ideas or work. Remember: karma is a you-know-what.
3. Thou shall not gossip, especially about the boss unless you want to be out of job.
4. Thou shall not snoop through your team members' desks or personal belongings. Mind your own business.
5. Thou shall not steal your departmental supplies, your coworker's lunch, or time off the clock. Theft is theft.
6. Thou shall not intimidate colleagues with blackmailing, bullying, or sexual harassment. Don't be a jerk.
7. Thou shall not use social media on days when you fake sick or make up doctors' appointments. Don't be stupid!
8. Thou shall not name drop to score a hookup, credibility, or date. It will come back to bite you.
9. Thou shall not lie. White lie, black lie, big lie, or small lie, they are all lies. And that includes half-truths too.
10. Thou shall not misuse company-issued devices. Just say no to sexting.

---

[74] Victoria Duff, "Examples of Unethical Behavior in the Workplace," *Houston Chronicle*, accessed May 14, 2014, http://smallbusiness.chron.com/examples-unethical-behavior-workplace-10092.html.

Taking Accountability Boundary Principle: The Right Way to Repair a Ruined Reputation

Keith Wyche said, "Forgiveness of others is really a gift to myself."[75]

If there is nothing else our culture loves more, it's a good comeback story. Even the worst mess makers have proven that you rise above mistakes. Those folks who haven't crossed the promised land of complete forgiveness will find that making it right takes time. In truth, as the saying goes, "Failure is not final." But when you find yourself in a personal crisis, the most important thing to do is forgive yourself first, according to spiritual life coach Iyanla Vanzant.

> Day one, forgive yourself. Forgive your thoughts, your beliefs, your judgments, and your feelings because every experience has that—a thought, a belief, a judgment, and a feeling. So when [forgive ourselves], the energy frees up in our body for us to do better.[76]

We all know that taking accountability is not easy. However, when you allow yourself to experience the journey of restoration, you allow your walls to come down and to let in forgiveness. Don't fight the process. At this point you have nothing more to lose. Be humble, transparent, and real. With a good action plan, you can find your way back:

- **Apologize.** You might not see an immediate positive response from saying "I'm sorry," but there is always power in asking for forgiveness. No matter how hard it is to say or what you think will or won't happen after you say it, it's a necessary aspect of your action plan that you cannot afford to ignore. The more genuine you come across, the better the chances that you will find redemption.
- **Disappear for a little while.** Once you apologize, give people room to breathe. Don't stalk them with calls or texts issuing

---

[75] Interview with Keith Wyche, March 10, 2015

[76] "Iyanla Vanzant Part 01," YouTube video, 11:34, posted by "Arise Entertainment 360," January 8, 2014, https://www.youtube.com/watch?v=2LvRbmcuVMQ.

additional apologies or shower them with acts of kindness. This will only give off the appearance of selfishness, the last impression you want to give someone who thinks you're already only concerned about yourself in the first place
- **Keep a journal.** Studies show that journaling is a strong therapeutic tool. Through writing we can channel our thoughts and feelings in a safe and healthy manner. While it's nice to confide in others, be careful that you don't create more problems rehashing the situation.
- **Do better.** Don't take on a victim mentality. Instead commit yourself to goals that will help you grow in weak areas and become an overall better person.

The Baby Boomer's Reaction: Image, What Others Think of You Matters

As a child it was instilled in me not to give too much credence to how others perceived me. As long as I knew who I was, what I stood for, and what I believed about myself, the opinions of others were of no consequence. I've hear it said recently that "others' opinion of you is none of your business." While on the surface I agree, particularly as it pertains to maintaining a healthy self-esteem, the raw reality is, in the work world, the opinions of others really do matter. The minute you step into the workplace, everything about you sends off signals to those around you. From your outer appearance and to how effectively you communicate and manage or mismanage your time, everything is noticed. Later these observations come into play when pay and promotions, rewards and recognition, and, most importantly, opportunities for growth are being decided.

Advice to Millennials

- News flash: everyone doesn't need to know everything about you!
- Behave as if anything you do or say publically will be on the six o'clock news. With today's smartphone technology, it just might!

- Never post any pictures, sayings, or comments on social media that reflect poorly on you or your organization.
- Remember: whether you like it or not, who you associate with says a great deal about who you are.

Advice to Boomers

- Be sensitive to the fact that these young professionals grew up in a "show all-tell all" world. As such, they might not be aware of the dangers of social media and way it can impact their brand.
- Be patient. Remember: you were young once!

Chapter 4

Good Is Still Not Enough

Don't Let Complacency Kill Your Career

Competition is one of the most craved addictions in the world. Man's innate infatuation with being the best, coupled with the rush of winning, pushes us to chase the high repeatedly. Much like Starbuck's coffee or Hershey's chocolate, its chronic dependency is both culturally celebrated and psychologically impossible to beat.

For many a millennial, one of our first tastes of competition occurs on the playground during the draft for grade school kickball or freeze tag games. You remember how it went down. Two team captains are summoned to select a squad of players to prove who dominated recess for the day. The remaining classmates found themselves crowded among each other, like a scene out of *Hunger Games*, hoping to be selected before the last (wo)man standing.

If you were a first-round draft pick, it represented your rank as a star athlete. Second-round picks were usually above average athletes but not as superior as the number-one pick. Anyone after that was probably a subpar player who may have gotten by on any connections he or she held in well-known cliques. But if you were the dead last pick in the draft, you were pretty much mocked as Mister (or Miss) Irrelevant. Ultimately the unspoken message that your peers projected to your subconscious was that your presence (being seen or noticed)[77] occupied little to no value on the team.

Worse than the social shame you endured were the emotional scars those humbling moments left behind, feelings of what legendary sportscaster Jim McKay summed up best as "the agony of defeat."[78] For a kid just wanting to fit in and have fun, that's a tough pill to swallow.

Yet as young adults, those humiliating feelings of inadequacy still haunt some of us as we tread along our career paths. Maybe those feelings didn't flare up from a childish game. Maybe it was from

- constantly being compared to someone you perceived was better than you were
- being passed over as MVP on your varsity team after tirelessly working to stand out
- having learning disabilities that led you to believe you weren't as smart as your peers were
- being waitlisted to attend your dream college
- enduring months of unemployment
- being rejected by a love interest

Or maybe it was just a little voice in your head telling you that you weren't good enough all these years.

Whatever the situation your delicate self-esteem became addicted to the stagnation of complacency instead of the stretching of competition.

---

[77] "Presence," Merriam-Webster, http://www.merriam-webster.com/dictionary/presence.

[78] Tom Cramer, "ABC's The Wide World Of Sports," Huffington Post, March 13, 2013, www.huffingtonpost.com/tom-cramer/wide-world-of-sports_b_2831708.html.

How the Comfort Zone of Complacency Becomes Dangerous

com·pla·cent *adjective* \kəm-'plā-sənt\: satisfied with how things are and not wanting to change them.

In his *Forbes* column, "10 Signs Your Employees Are Growing Complacent in Their Careers," contributor Glenn Llopis shared the sentiments of an unnamed Fortune 500 executive who shared how complacency ate away at his ambitions. "I am burned out and tired of the nonsense. I am not inspired to put in the extra hours … I just do my job well, play the political game, smile and get my check."[79]

Have you felt like that about a job before? You just show up, smile, and get a check? I've been there. During my freshman year at the University of Toledo, I worked at an off-campus fast-food seafood restaurant with my best friend Kali. I won't speak for both of us, but I will say I hated every single second of that job. We were always short-staffed. The franchise owners were very frank with their thoughts on minorities. The customers were often rude. Let's not even talk about the food prep process. At the end of the day, it was a means to an end, and I showed, smiled, and got my check, like the Fortune 500 executive above.

That experience is why I always treat retail and food service professionals with the utmost respect. I know what it's like to be on the other side. After all there is no sadder existence in this world than being employed in a job that literally sucks the life out of you. Yet in this turbulent economy, we've learned to embrace the saving grace of a steady paycheck whether we're crazy about what we do or not. However, Llopis warns of the dangers of chasing paper without the passion to support it.

1. **We grow disengaged.** The danger: By checking out, we become lost in the clouds, working fewer hours and only doing just enough to get the job done.

---

[79] Glenn Llopis, "10 Signs Your Employees Are Growing Complacent in Their Careers," *Forbes*, July 8, 2013 (9:45 AM), http://www.forbes.com/sites/glennllopis/2013/07/08/10-signs-your-employees-are-growing-complacent-in-their-careers.

2. **We stop thinking.** The danger: By just going with the flow, we are on the path of being unproductive and unknowingly shut off the valves of our value creation.
3. **We stop taking initiative.** The danger: By not taking the lead on assigned tasks, we lose mental toughness, and our presence becomes more of a distraction as our attitude begins to bring down the team.
4. **We stop investing in ourselves.** The danger: By losing our drive to be high performers, we willfully close ourselves out to opportunities for learning and networking, two career-enhancing components our professional development cannot survive without.
5. **We are not managing our personal brands.** The danger: By lacking awareness of our perception, we have put our personal brands on life support.
6. **We take shortcuts.** The danger: By not being thorough or detail-oriented, we become disruptive to the corporate culture and a liability to the organization we serve.
7. **We don't take risks.** The danger: By only doing what we're told to do, rather than becoming a more integral and influential part of the team, our careers get stalled in the sidelines.
8. **We lose our passion.** The danger: By no longer getting excited about our responsibilities or work, it becomes impossible for us to achieve any level of career success.
9. **We become disgruntled with our current career destinations.** The danger: By failing to take full accountability for our poor decision-making, we play the victim role.
10. **We lose hope for a brighter future.** The danger: By losing hope, we've hit rock bottom.[80]

Do you see the trend here? Over time complacency becomes a cancer eating away at our performance, exposure, and perception, leaving our supervisors with only one solution, termination.

---

[80] Ibid.

Detouring from the Danger Zone of Mediocrity

Dr. Seuss said, "Only you can control your future."[81]

Some of the realest lessons on competition and complacency are illustrated best through the whimsical storytelling of iconic writer Dr. Seuss. Believe it or not, the beloved children's author and illustrator didn't find writing success easily. In fact twenty-seven publishers rejected his first children's book, *And to Think That I Saw It on Mulberry Street*. It was finally published in 1937 when Dr. Seuss was thirty-three. In fact he was all ready to burn the manuscript, but his former Dartmouth classmate-turned-publisher purchased the rights to the book. He went on to illustrate and write forty-four children's books like *Green Eggs and Ham, Horton Hears a Who!, Oh, the Places You'll Go,* and *How the Grinch Stole Christmas*. He won Academy Awards, a Peabody, and the Pulitzer Prize. And his books have been translated into more than twenty languages and sold six hundred million copies worldwide. Dr. Seuss passed away in 1991 when he was eighty-seven, but his quotes continue to inspire.[82]

While his prose was catered to feeding children's imagination, there's no doubt that professionals can take his words to heart as well.

- *"Oh the things YOU can find, if YOU don't stay behind!"* The view from behind is not a very good view, as the person in front of you is blocking most of it. So get out in front and face things head-on. You'll find that it's much more fascinating and there is plenty more to see.
- *"And will YOU succeed? Yes YOU will indeed! (98 and 3/4 percent guaranteed.)"* Of course there are no 100 percent guarantees in life, but when you have a positive mind-set like the one this quote instills, you have a pretty good shot at getting it right. Success begins in the mind, and if you go in with a

---

[81] Jasmine Barta, "13 Dr. Seuss quotes to live by," http://college.usatoday.com/2013/07/11/13-dr-seuss-quotes-to-live-by.

[82] Jeryl Brunner, "On the 100th Anniversary of Dr. Seuss's Birth His Quotes Continue to Inspire," Huffington Post, May 4, 2014, http://www.huffingtonpost.com/jeryl-brunner/on-the-100th-anniversary-_b_4891306.html.

defeatist attitude, you'll surely come up short. Just think of what you could accomplish if you had the belief that you would succeed. You don't need to be completely assured of success. It's good to have a bit of a possibility of failure, or it wouldn't be interesting. Just go into it with the confidence that there's a high chance of success for you.

- *"YOU are YOU. Now, isn't that pleasant?"* You have to be comfortable in your own skin, and this reminds us that it's great to be ourselves. There's no one else we can possibly be, and it's a pleasant thought to think that it's pleasant to be yourself. Being happy to be you is key to a happy existence, and it really doesn't make any sense to be less than pleased to be you. There isn't any way to be anyone else, but if there are things about yourself that you don't really like, you can make changes to improve yourself.
- *"Why fit in when YOU were born to stand out?"* Standing out can come in many forms. You can give a standout performance, or you can simply hold ideas and beliefs that are uncommon and go against the grain. So don't be content just to do things the way everyone else is doing it. Stand out like you were meant to!
- *"YOU have brains in your head. YOU have feet in your shoes. YOU can steer yourself in any direction YOU choose."* Determining your destination is priority one. What the brain can dream up, the body can fulfill as long as there is a strong determination and a clear vision of what it is that is wanted. The great part is that this is all up to you. You have plenty of choices, and you can head in countless directions.
- *"The more that YOU read, the more things YOU will know. The more that YOU learn, the more places you'll go."* Leaders are readers, no doubt about that. Reading helps you learn about whatever you want to know about. You can study up on an exotic travel destination or a new method of doing business. There will always be those willing to share their knowledge with you, and this gives you a jump on the situation so you can have as much information as possible. Reading and learning really are the ticket to getting around the globe.

- *"You'll miss the best things if YOU keep your eyes shut."* Don't be afraid to keep your eyes open and take it all in. There is much to be seen, but if your eyes are closed, you'll miss it. In the story Seuss says that there are plenty of things to learn about, so he may be referring to the fact that there's so much in the world to discover. But many of us don't bother to learn about it, so it's the equivalent of going through life with our eyes shut. It could be a way of saying we need to rekindle that love of learning and start discovering the world like we did when we were children.
- *"Think left and think right and think low and think high. Oh, the things YOU can think up if only YOU try!"* It's funny to think about thinking. It seems like it's something that just happens on autopilot and not something that you can control. Realizing that you're actually in control of your thoughts and you can think deep, not-so-deep, happy, or sad thoughts on command, it becomes clear that it's your responsibility to think the thoughts you want to think. Seuss seems to be encouraging you to think in all sorts of different ways and directions so you can scour the mind for really amazing ideas.
- *"You're on your own. And YOU know what YOU know. And YOU are the one who'll decide where to go."* It can sometimes be overwhelming to think that you're on your own in the world, but at the same time, it gives you the freedom to choose your own path. You've amassed some knowledge at this point, and you are making decisions based on that knowledge. No one else will be able to make your decisions for you, no matter how much advice you get. You'll ultimately be the one that chooses where you'll end up.
- *"Today YOU are YOU, that is truer than true. There is no one alive who is you-er than YOU."* This is one of the most popular quotes by Dr. Seuss, and perhaps it's because it's so true and it's such a witty way of saying it. There really isn't anyone out there that's more you than you are. It's something that can be said about you for your entire life. No one else can think for you, do

your work for you, and experience happiness for you. It's all up to you, and you put your own mark on your life.[83]

When In Doubt, Just W.O.W.

Those who are experts at exemplifying their competitive edge understand the most important rule of the game. When in doubt, just W.O.W. The W.O.W. Principle is grounded in my dad's famous philosophy that "good is not enough" except in doing "what others won't." There are only two rules: be purposeful and create value.

Keith Battle said, "Whatever you're born to do, you'll soar at. But whatever you're doing that's wrong you'll be sour at."[84] During a visit to the DC-Maryland-Virginia area last year, I heard a powerful message on the subject of purpose delivered by Reverend Keith Battle, pastor of Zion Church in Bowie, Maryland. Throughout his sermon, "When Preparation Meets Opportunity," Reverend Battle outlined three attributes that define people who operate in their purpose. When you're in your purpose, he says the following:

- Not only do you identify problems, you help solve them.
- You exceed expectations.
- You stun others with your excellence.

Keith Battle said, "If you are a person who only wants to do just enough to get by, just what your job description says, and just what your purview of responsibilities says, then you're not in your purpose."[85]

Purpose-Identifying Questions

- What is it that you do that, when you do it, you go from the level of good to the level of great when you do it? Here's the caveat.

---

[83] "37 Dr. Seuss Quotes That Can Change the World," Bright Drops, accessed July 2, 2014, http://brightdrops.com/dr-seuss-quotes.

[84] Pastor Keith Battle, "When Preparation Meets Opportunity (Sermon)," Zion Church, Bowie, MD.

[85] Ibid.

It can't just be you who thinks you're exceptional at it. Others have had to say. You're the bomb at that.
- What is that thing you do that, when you do it and you do it exceptionally and other people say you do it exceptionally when you do it, you come alive inside? You get excited when you know you have the opportunity to do it.

Now let's put it all together and look at an example of someone who W.O.W.ed her way to work for Warren Buffett. Tracy Britt Cool said, "Following my instincts, taking the path less traveled, and leaning in before my career even began definitely paid off."[86] With beauty, brains, and bravado, Tracy Britt Cool is a certified boss. Not a "boss" in baby boomer verbiage but like the "boss" lauded in the lyrics of the 2009 R&B single "She Got Her Own" by Ne-Yo featuring Jamie Foxx and Fabolous.

She don't slow down 'cause she ain't got time
To be complaining, shawty gon' shine
Independent queen workin' for her throne[87]

If you're not in the know, you may be wondering who Tracy Britt Cool is. What throne is she governing? And why should I care? Lean in and learn.

In high school Britt Cool was voted most likely to become a billionaire.[88] Today the millennial mogul is making major boss moves as the right-hand woman to one of the world's most respected billionaires, Warren Buffett.

If you think her story will read like just another trust fund kid handed success on platter, you're wrong. Britt Cool grew up on a farm in Manhattan. Manhattan, Kansas, that is, where her parents ran Britt's

---

[86] "Tracy Britt, Financial Assistant," www.leanin.org/stories/tracy-britt.

[87] Antonia Jiminez, John Jackson, Shaffer Smith, David Brown, and Donna Summer, "She Got Her Own" (MP3 Audio File) from *Year of the Gentleman*, http://www.metrolyrics.com/she-got-her-own-lyrics-neyo.html, accessed August 18, 2014.

[88] Noah Buhayar and Laura Colby, "Buffett Leans on 29 Year Old Cool to Oversee Problems," Bloomberg, January 21, 2014, http://www.bloomberg.com/news/2014-01-21/buffett-leans-on-29-year-old-cool-to-oversee-problems.html.

Garden Acres, growing fruit, vegetables, and flowers. It wasn't Wall Street, but this is where Britt honed her business skills and developed her work ethic.[89]

By the time Britt Cool arrived in Omaha, Nebraska, in 2009 to meet with Warren Buffett, she brought her Harvard MBA, a glittering résumé, and a boatload of ambition. But she also brought the famed investor a gift to highlight their shared Midwestern roots: a bushel of corn and a batch of tomatoes. The seeds she planted that day yielded quick results, a job as Mr. Buffett's financial assistant.[90] As it's written her success sounds pretty much like instant success. In truth it was not. The reality, in the words of rapper Meek Mill, is that there were levels to rise from Ivy Leaguer to corporate leader.

In a personal essay penned for LeanIn.org, Britt Cool shared the realities of her rise from Ivy Leaguer to corporate leader.

- **She cast her vision as CEO of her career early on.** She said, "I knew early on that I wanted to work in the investment field."[91] From the very beginning, Britt was focused. While others were partying in college, she chose to spend her free time studying up on finance and her summers working on Wall Street. Upon graduation, rather than take a job offer right away, Brit opted to go straight to business school and earn her MBA.
- **She took calculated risks to reap long-term results.** Her decision to attend business school without at least a few years of real world experience was risky. Many naysayers warned her that it would be a mistake and she would reduce her chances to find gainful employment later on. However, Brit was willing to bet on herself. Furthermore she didn't want to get too comfortable

---

[89] "The New Warren Buffett: Billionaire 'is grooming 28-year-old Harvard grad to take his place when he retires'," *Daily Mail Online*, June 12, 2013, http://www.dailymail.co.uk/news/article-2340569/Meet-28-year-old-Tracy-Britt-Harvard-grad-Warren-Buffett-grooming-place-retires.html#ixzz3Am8apb1b.

[90] Anupreeta Das, "A Rising Star Emerges from Berkshire," *Wall Street Journal*, June 11, 2013, http://online.wsj.com/news/articles/SB10001424127887324904004578539443761846024.

[91] "Tracy Britt, Financial Assistant," www.leanin.org/stories/tracy-britt.

with a job, as she might not have been motivated to complete business school.
- **She accepted feedback and admitted her flaws.** After being accepted into Harvard Business School, she learned, in her class of nine hundred, she was one of only eight direct admits who entered the program without having worked beforehand. One of her fellow classmates made her aware of the reality, upon graduation, she would be competing with classmates who were older and had work experience and more credibility. Britt accepted the feedback and actually became even more determined.
- **She was grateful**. Britt recognizes how fortunate she is to work as a financial assistant to Warren Buffett, one of the world's wealthiest individuals. She is grateful for his mentoring, support, and opportunity to learn from an investment icon. While she may not know what the future holds, she is off to a great start, and her gamble seems to have paid off.

The Baby Boomer's Reaction: Your A-game, Never Leave Home without It!

The older I get, the more I have come to realize that most of us are satisfied about just getting a passing grade. We live life as if it's a pass-fail outcome, where the benefits of working smarter, exceeding expectations, and doing one's best aren't worth the effort. Consequently most of us also live mediocre, "me too," "good enough for government work" lives that never tap into our true potential, never realize our achievable goals, and never enjoy the satisfaction that comes from being all you can be. This is particularly true when it comes to being continuous learners.

For most, learning stops after that diploma, degree, MBA, or last promotion. In reality learning is a lifelong event. As I think back on those who have enjoyed the most success, regardless of their field of endeavor, I envision those who maintained a healthy intellectual curiosity about life. This thirst and hunger for knowledge by the few who desire it has brought us more technological, medical, and other advancements than all the good-enough efforts combined.

Advice to Millennials

- Avoid the temptation to accept the status quo, either personally or professionally.
- Understand that reaching your potential will require effort, dedication, determination, and focus. There are no elevators to success; you have to take the stairs.
- Stay current to remain relevant. Learning doesn't end at graduation. Make a habit of staying on top of business/industry trends, economic impacts, and current events on a daily basis. Also make an effort to read at least four business-related or meaningful nonfiction books a year.
- Bring your A-game every day!

Advice to Boomers

- Never lower your expectations for millennials. They are capable of more than you can imagine, even if they don't want to admit it.
- Encourage and support their efforts to learn, develop, and grow. Don't try to limit them or hold them to the same career timetables that you encountered thirty-plus years ago. They learn differently and at a faster pace that most of us are used to.
- Don't let their brashness and cockiness blind you to the potential and creativity they bring to the table. As they begin to acquire business maturity, humility will balance them out.

Chapter 5

Don't Get Caught in the Catfish Culture

Social Media Does Not Replace Social Interaction

Mackensie Smith, blogger at TheNextWeb.com, said "Millennials are a generation of tweeting, SnapChatting, friending, checking-in, texting, selfie-taking, diverse individuals interweaving the Webs of cultivated collective online profiles. Digital use is not just an action … it's a lifestyle."[92]

How deep does your love run for technology run? Research shows that many millennials' infatuation borderlines insanity. According to the Truth About Youth global study, when given a list of things (including their cosmetics, car, passport, phone, and sense of smell) and told they could only save two, 53 percent of millennials would give up their own

---

[92] McCann Worldwide, "The Truth about Youth," Scribd.com, May 2011, http://www.scribd.com/doc/56263899/McCann-Worldgroup-Truth-About-Youth.

sense of smell if it meant they could keep an item of technology, most often their phone or laptop.[93] We all know how important technology is, but a willingness to sacrifice one's human senses to keep it shows just how intrinsic it has become.

Perhaps it's not all that surprising when you consider that technology represents all the friends you could ever want, all the knowledge you will ever need, and all the entertainment you could desire. Technology is more than a useful tool or an enabler. It is truly our fifth sense.

Millennials sees technology as Play-Doh, something they use in an utterly malleable and instinctive way. Baby boomers start with, "What will this box allow me to do?" Gen Y starts with, "What do I want to do? Where can my imagination take me?"[94]

Millennials Interrupted

How many times have you ever found yourself caught between a smartphone and an awkward social situation:

- Cuddling with your significant other only to be sidelined by their smartphone
- Scheduling dinner and drinks with your besties, only to have them block your conversation to catch up on their newsfeeds they've probably been scanning all day
- Taking a trip to be at one with your mate, only to find yourself feeling like the third wheel to his or her telephone call about nothing
- Wishing you could slap that one friend who makes a photo shoot out of every outing
- Dishing out your last dime to attend your favorite artist's concert, only to be blinded by a sea of cell phone cameras capturing every minute

A 2013 viral video, "I Forgot My Phone," depicts these scenes with one jarring, all-too-familiar addition, cell phones, according to a *Wall*

---

[93] Ibid.

[94] Ibid.

Street Journal article. Running to just over two minutes, the video isn't showing us anything we haven't seen before or experienced ourselves. But it seems to have hit a nerve, garnering nearly fifty million views since it launched on YouTube on August 22.

How often are you on your cell phone, and when is it time to put away your phone? In an age of Facebook, Twitter, and Google Glass, is it possible to live in the moment without Instagramming it?[95]

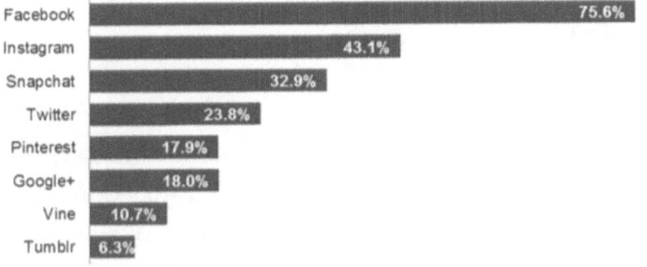

As we learned from the Truth About Youth study and the anecdote above, millennials' deep relationship with technology is shaping our attitudes toward community.[97] Many fear this attitude will impair our ability to effectively engage in formal social interactions.

A study conducted for online casino Yazino found that one in four people spend more time socializing online via sites such as Facebook and Twitter than they do in person. Additionally, even when there is an opportunity to see people face-to-face, on weekends, for example, up

---

[95] Lara Day, "Viral Video: I Forgot My Phone," *Wall Street Journal*, August 8, 2013, http://blogs.wsj.com/scene/2013/08/26/viral-video-i-forgot-my-phone.

[96] Sarah Perez, "Snapchat is now the #3 Social App Among Millennials," Tech Crunch, August 11, 2014, http://techcrunch.com/2014/08/11/snapchat-is-now-the-3-social-app-among-millennials.

[97] McCann Worldwide, "The Truth about Youth," Scribd.com, May 2011, http://www.scribd.com/doc/56263899/McCann-Worldgroup-Truth-About-Youth.

to 11 percent of adults still prefer to stay at home and communicate on their devices instead.[98]

Rise of the Corporate Catfish Culture

Used as a verb, "catfish" means to pretend to be someone you're not online. And what happens to a millennial who doesn't develop his or her social skills? They risk becoming corporate catfish.

Millennial filmmaker and MTV personality Neve Schulman coined the term "catfishing," which describes someone who dupes another via social media. In some ways Schulman says we all are catfish in the sense that we create a version of ourselves.

> We have the power to present the version (of ourselves) we would like people to see, and because of the system that is in place now with social media—the currency of 'likes' and the value of appealing to the most people … we've all started to crave and almost become addicted to that external appreciation and attention and sort of being liked.[99]

The danger of being caught in the catfish culture is that the digital identity you project online doesn't translate in person when you have to sell the persona you penned on paper.

You Can't Filter a Poor Personality

Shooting yourself at the right angle, in the best light, and with the right filter can take you from basic to Beyoncé or boring to Beckham

---

[98] Jasmine Fowlkes, "Viewpoint: Why Social Media Is Destroying Social Skills," *USA Today*, November 11, 2012, http://college.usatoday.com/2012/10/11/opinion-why-social-media-is-destroying-our-social-skills.

[99] Jennifer Weigel, "Keeping it Real: Nev Schulman, Host of MTV's Catfish Weighs In on Shaky World of Online Identities," *Chicago Tribune*, September 2, 2014, http://www.chicagotribune.com/lifestyles/sc-fam-0902-schulman-catfish-20140902-story.html#page=1.

in a matter of seconds. Unfortunately in the real world, where effective communication is king, there are no filters to fake soft skills.

According to recent research findings from CareerBuilder, a majority of employers (77 percent) believe soft skills (qualitative skills such as interpersonal dependability or savvy) are just as important as hard skills (quantitative skills such as foreign language fluency or technical proficiency).[100] Rosemary Haefner, vice president of human resources at CareerBuilder, a leading jobs resource and posting site, said,

> When Companies are assessing job candidates, they're looking for the best of both worlds—someone who is not only proficient in a particular function but who also has the right personality. Along with responsibilities, it's important to highlight soft skills that can give employers an idea of how quickly you can adapt and solve problems, whether you can be relied on to follow through and how effectively you can lead and motivate others.[101]

How to Sharpen Your Soft Skills

What distinguishes good communicators from great communicators? According to *Forbes* contributor Mike Myatt, the answer lies in their heightened sense of situational and contextual awareness.[102] The best communicators are great listeners and astute in their observations. Great communicators are skilled at reading a person/group by sensing the moods, dynamics, attitudes, values, and concerns of those being communicated with. Not only do they read their environment well, they possess the uncanny ability to adapt their messaging to said environment without missing a beat. The message is not about the messenger; it has nothing to do with the messenger. It is, however,

---

[100] Janell Hazelwood, "Soft Skills, Hard Success," *Black Enterprise*, July/August 2014, 44.

[101] Ibid.

[102] Mike Myatt, "10 Communication Secrets of Great Leaders," *Forbes*, April 4, 2012, http://www.forbes.com/sites/mikemyatt/2012/04/04/10-communication-secrets-of-great-leaders.

100 percent about meeting the needs and expectations of those you're communicating with.

So how do you know when your skills have matured to the point where you've become an excellent communicator? The answer is that you'll have reached the point where your interactions with others consistently use the following eleven principles.

1. **Speak not with a forked tongue.** In most cases people just won't open up to those they don't trust. When people have a sense a leader is worthy of their trust, they will invest time and take risks in ways they never would if their leader had a reputation built upon poor character or lack of integrity. While you can attempt to demand trust, it rarely works. Trust is best created by earning it with right behavior, thinking, and decision-making. Keep in mind that people will forgive many things where trust exists but will rarely forgive anything where trust is absent.
2. **Get personal.** Stop issuing corporate communications and begin having organizational conversations. Think dialogue, not monologue. Here's the thing. The more personal and engaging the conversation is, the more effective it will be. There is great truth in the axiom, "People don't care how much you know until they know how much you care." Classic business theory tells leaders to stay at arm's length. I say you stay at arm's length if you want to remain in the dark, receiving only highly sanitized versions of the truth. If you don't develop meaningful relationships with people, you'll never know what's really on their minds until it's too late to do anything about it.
3. **Get specific.** Eleven times out of ten, specificity is better than ambiguity. Learn to communicate with clarity. Simple and concise is always better than complicated and confusing. Time has never been a more precious commodity than it is today. It is critical leaders learn how to cut to the chase and hit the high points. It's also important to expect the same from others. Without understanding the value of brevity and clarity, it is unlikely you'll ever be afforded the opportunity to get to the granular level, as people will tune you out long before you ever

get there. Your goal is to weed out the superfluous and make your words count.

4. **Focus on the leave-behinds, not the takeaways.** Not only are the best communicators skilled at learning and gathering information while communicating, they are also adept at transferring ideas, aligning expectations, inspiring action, and spreading their vision. The key is to approach each interaction with a servant's heart. When you truly focus on contributing more than receiving, you will have accomplished the goal. Even though this may seem counterintuitive, by intensely focusing on the other party's wants, needs, and desires, you'll learn far more than you ever would by focusing on your agenda.

5. **Have an open mind.** I've often said that the rigidity of a closed mind is the single greatest limiting factor of new opportunities. A leader takes his or her game to a whole new level the minute he or she willingly seeks out those who hold dissenting opinions and opposing positions with the goal of not convincing them to change their minds but with the objective of understanding what's on their mind. I'm always amazed at how many people are truly fearful of opposing views when they should be genuinely curious and interested. Open dialogues with those who confront, challenge, stretch, and develop you. Remember: it's not the opinion that matters but rather the willingness to discuss it with an open mind and learn.

6. **Shut up and listen.** Great leaders know when to dial it up, down, and off (mostly down and off). Simply broadcasting your message ad nauseum will not have the same result as engaging in meaningful conversation, but this assumes that you understand that the greatest form of discourse takes place within a conversation and not a lecture or a monologue. When you reach that point in your life where the light bulb goes off and you begin to understand that knowledge is not gained by flapping your lips but by removing your earwax, you have taken the first step to becoming a skilled communicator.

7. **Replace ego with empathy.** I have long advised leaders not to let their ego write checks that their talent can't cash. When candor

is communicated with empathy and caring and not the prideful arrogance of an overinflated ego, good things begin to happen. Empathetic communicators display a level of authenticity and transparency that is not present with those who choose to communicate behind the carefully crafted façade propped up by a very fragile ego. Understanding this communication principle helps turn anger into respect and doubt into trust.

8. **Read between the lines.** Take a moment and reflect back on any great leader that comes to mind. You'll find that he or she is very adept at reading between the lines. He or she has the uncanny ability to understand what is not said, witnessed, or heard. Being a leader should not be viewed as a license to increase the volume of rhetoric. Rather astute leaders know that there is far more to be gained by surrendering the floor than filibustering. In this age of instant communication, everyone seems to be in such a rush to communicate what's on his or her mind that he or she fails to realize everything to be gained from the minds of others. If you keep your eyes and ears open and your mouth shut, you'll be amazed at how your level or organizational awareness is raised.

9. **When you speak, know what you're talking about.** Develop a technical command over your subject matter. If you don't possess subject matter expertise, few people will give you the time of day. Most successful people have little interest in listening to those individuals who cannot add value to a situation or topic but force themselves into a conversation just to hear themselves speak. The fake-it-until-you-make-it days have long since passed, and for most people I know, fast and slick equals not credible. You've all heard the saying, "It's not what you say but how you say it that matters." And while there is surely an element of truth in that statement, I'm here to tell you that it matters very much what you say. Good communicators address both the what and how aspects of messaging so they don't fall prey to becoming the smooth talker who leaves people with the impression of form over substance.

10. **Speak to groups as individuals.** Leaders don't always have the luxury of speaking to individuals in an intimate setting. Great communicators can tailor a message so they can speak to ten people in a conference room or ten thousand people in an auditorium and have them feel as if they were speaking directly to each one of them as an individual. Knowing how to work a room and establish credibility, trust, and rapport are keys to successful interactions.
11. **Be prepared to change the message if needed.** Another component of communications strategy that is rarely discussed is how to prevent a message from going bad and what to do when does. It's called being prepared and developing a contingency plan. Again you must keep in mind, for successful interactions to occur, your objective must align with those you are communicating with. If your expertise, empathy, clarity, and so forth don't have the desired effect, which is very rare by the way, you need to be able to make an impact by changing things up on the fly. Use great questions, humor, stories, analogies, relevant data, and, where needed, bold statements to help connect and engender the confidence and trust that it takes for people to want to engage. While it is sometimes necessary to shock and awe, this tactic should be reserved as a last resort.[103]

The Baby Boomer's Reaction: I Thought Catfish Was Something You Eat

It's an understatement that most baby boomers don't embrace social media the way millennials do. While most of us are just getting comfortable with Twitter, Instagram, and the thousands of apps that exist, our younger millennial counterparts can manage most of their life from their smartphone. However, what I have observed is, while they have mastered the use of technology, they struggle mightily in developing and cultivating relationships interpersonally. They tend to hide behind technology, choosing to send an instant message versus

---

[103] Ibid.

picking up the phone. They would rather tweet and send text messages, as opposed to getting up and walking down the hallway to meet face-to-face with a colleague. As such it is quite possible to have an online persona that is bigger than life when, in reality, they struggle to hold a meaningful conversation.

The millennials that will rise the fastest and go the farthest are those who work on their interpersonal communication skills. Additionally they should learn how to work effectively with all types of coworkers from the introverts to the extroverts, the jovial to the stoic, and those that look like them and those who are different.

Advice to Millennials

- Put down the smartphone and embrace personal interaction.
- Stop sending instant messages and text messages, and grab a cup of coffee with a colleague to discuss a project.
- Take a course online, or read up on the various personality types, as you will most assuredly meet and have to work with all types.
- Look for opportunities to engage one-on-one to truly develop working relationships with your coworkers. This way they get to meet and know you, not your online persona.

Advice to Boomers

- Don't be afraid to keep up with the latest social media technology, not to become an expert but to at least be conversant and better relate to your younger associates.
- Be proactive in engaging millennials and force them out of their comfort zone.
- Look for teachable moments to coach millennials and relay the importance of interpersonal skills in the workplace.

Chapter 6

So You Want to Be a Boss

Learn How to Be a Leader First

My father likes to wax nostalgic about his early career. After graduating from college, he began his career as a sales representative with Ohio Bell, part of the AT&T family. He was by far the youngest member of his team, and his much older coworkers gave him the nickname "College Boy." He recalls having to earn his stripes before his peers took him seriously. He ran the errands, made the lunch reservations, typed the meeting agendas, and did basically whatever grunt work needed to be done. In time, about three years actually, he was finally accepted into the group. It was the old days when seniority was king, so career advancement was more about waiting your turn as opposed to being a meritocracy.

It took my father over ten years to earn his first real management role, one where he was not only given responsibility for managing people but helping create strategy, owning the profit and loss of the department, and serving basically as the boss.

However, my father came of age during the early eighties. It was a time of minimal technology. (Personal computers were a pipe dream.) Theory X management styles ("do as I say or else") and group think were the norm. It was very little innovation, minimal utilization of technology, and militaristic organization structures where career advancement was very linear in nature.

This is not the new reality. Millennials enter the workplace wanting to make a meaningful contribution on day one. We want to be taken seriously for the value we bring immediately, not in ten years. We aren't satisfied just running errands, getting the coffee, and helping others understand the latest app. And while we understand and appreciate hierarchy, we don't want to work for bosses. We want to work for leaders. And equally as important, we want to become leaders, not just bosses.

Old School Career Advancement

When it comes to the old school game of career advancement, baby boomers were unofficially categorized as one of two types of players: creeps and connectors. Disclaimer: this is my theory including the made-up names used to illustrate my point.

Connectors, as you will read, have a positive perception. Creeps, on the contrary, carry a negative connotation. However, I'm sure it's a far less harsher title/expletive I know our parents probably used to describe their disgust for the slackers they encountered throughout their careers. Follow me here.

Creeps were leeches; convenience was their mode of manipulation. They conveniently

- met the minimum expectations mapped out in their job description
- asked for a raise or promotion without demonstrating a willingness to take on responsibilities that demand increased effort and visibility

- adorned their team player hat when they needed help and conveniently disappeared when it was time to pay it forward
- took advantage of company resources without considering how it's impacting the bottom line
- ran from the opportunities to grow and learn from constructive feedback.

Connectors were leaders; consistency was their calling card. They consistently:

- took initiative to perform and deliver beyond the expectations established in their roles
- welcomed new challenges to prove their competency and influence before pursuing advancement
- stepped up to support and work with their team members
- approached company resources with a budget-conscious attitude
- sought opportunities to receive and benefit from constructive feedback

So you're probably wondering what the fate was of the creep versus the connector. I'll let you in on a little secret. They both got talked about behind closed doors. But one was more likely to burn bridges, while the other was more likely to build allies. Can you guess which player your parent was/probably is?

Case Study: Career Advancement in the Millennial World

Now as we consider the twenty-first century game of career advancement, we have to understand, for baby boomers, it's no longer creeps versus connectors. It's us against them. Yes, we, the millennial body, are the new threat. But here's the thing. As much as we don't always see eye to eye with our elders, we have to accept one crucial fact. We still need them, and they need us. Yes, the business world is evolving, and if they want to survive, they need us. Similarly there is still a blueprint to business that we can't ignore, and if we're going to get ahead, we need them to help us too.

Now before we start fleshing out the details of putting our careers on the fast track, I want to take a moment to share findings that highlight our perception in the workplace. In 2013 PricewaterhouseCoopers (PwC), the University of Southern California, and the London Business School released the findings on an unprecedented study of a two-year, global study of millennials in the marketplace. The origins of the study stemmed from a crisis that many companies are facing today, retaining millennial talent.

A decade after the first millennials entered the halls of PwC, the company began to notice that the youngest generation of professionals were leaving in growing numbers after just a few years. Additionally and perhaps even more alarmingly, a significant majority of them appeared to lack interest in the traditional professional career path, one that required an intense work commitment early in their career in exchange to make partner later on.

PwC knew it needed to clarify the impact of what appeared to be a shift in culture. Consequently PwC undertook a massive generational study, the largest of its kind to better understand the attitudes and goals of its millennial workforce. Here's what they found:[104]

- **Many millennial employees are unconvinced that excessive work demands are worth the sacrifice to their personal life.** While working through and excelling during such demanding times can have significant rewards on an employee's future career (e.g., rapid skill development and advancement within the firm), millennials are largely convinced that what they would have to give up is worth such a sacrifice. Millennials value work/life balance, and the majority of them are unwilling to commit to making their work lives an exclusive priority, even with the promise of substantial compensation later on.
- **Millennials want more flexibility.** If they were able to make their current job more flexible, 64 percent of millennials would like to occasionally work from home, and 66 percent would

---

[104] Ann Donovan and Dennis Finn, "PwC's NextGen: A Global Generational Study," PwC, accessed March 31, 2014, http://www.pwc.com/en_GX/gx/hr-management-services/pdf/pwc-nextgen-study-2013.pdf.

like to shift their work hours. For their part, millennials do not believe that productivity should be measured by the number of hours worked at the office, but by the output of the work performed. They view work as a thing and not a place.

- **Millennials value collaboration and rewards.** Millennials place a high priority on workplace culture and desire a work environment that emphasizes teamwork and a sense of community. They also value transparency, especially as it relates to decisions about their careers, compensation, and rewards. Specifically, 41 percent of millennials prefer to be rewarded or recognized for their work at least monthly, if not more frequently, whereas 30 percent of non-millennials would like that level of frequency.

- **Many but not all stereotypes about millennials are untrue.** Despite a reputation perhaps to the contrary, the millennial generation of workers share some similarities with older generations in the workplace. They have grown up not expecting their organizations to meet all of their needs, including job security, and don't see themselves working for one organization for their entire careers. Although millennials have a natural aptitude for electronic forms of communication, email and social media platforms are not always their communication vehicles of choice, especially when it comes to discussions with their managers about their careers. Also while a common perception exists that millennials are not as committed or hardworking as their more senior colleagues, the study effectively busted this myth by revealing that millennials are as equally committed to their work.

- **Millennial attitudes are not totally universal, although there is significantly commonality between the United States/ Canada and Western Europe.** The global study found notable similarities and differences among millennials throughout the world. For example, millennial workers in every PwC firm around the world aspire to have greater work/life balance. However, the issue is particularly important for millennials in the more developed economies of North America and Europe and in the East region, where work/life balance has a stronger bearing on turnover, commitment, and job satisfaction than in other parts of the world. Additionally we discovered in a few countries where there is a strong differentiated culture that cultural norms can trump millennial views that surfaced elsewhere in the world. Millennial workers in East region countries also place a higher value on information about which assignments will enhance their development than do their non-millennial colleagues.

- **While the same basic drivers of retention exist for both millennials and non-millennials, their relative importance varies with millennials placing a greater emphasis on being supported and appreciated.** The NextGen study revealed, while the reasons for staying or leaving the firm are virtually the same between both millennials and non-millennials, their relative importance differs. Millennials have a greater expectation to be supported and appreciated in return for their contributions and to be part of a cohesive team. Flexibility in where they work and how much they work is also a key driver in millennial satisfaction. This view differs in importance from that of the non-millennial generation, which places greater importance on pay and development opportunities. Millennials in developed countries also expect PwC to create a work environment that allows them to thrive both personally and professionally.[105]

Now that we have a clear and unbiased perspective of our perception, let's take a quick moment to exhale a sigh of relief. Ah, yes. It's actually quite refreshing to be told that we're not that bad after all. In fact we do have worth and value in the marketplace. We do bring a special sauciness that can't be bottled up and replicated by baby boomers, and all we want is a little appreciation and recognition. Is that too much to ask for? Depending on whom you ask, yes.

---

[105] Ibid.

Work Habits That Work in Your Career Advancement Favor

Many millennials are successful at getting hired, but our baby boomer critics are convinced we don't know how to play the game. According to George Mason University professor Robert Deitz, they're kind of right.

> It is simply not true that those (i.e. Gen Y) professionals with the 'best,' the flashiest, resumes, meaning those who attended the most prestigious colleges and graduate schools, have earned the highest grades, have held the niftiest internships inevitably rise to the top of their professions. There are many other qualities, few of which are taught in school, that lead to success in the workplace.[106]

In his role as a talent management consultant to Fortune 500 companies, my father, Keith Wyche, often shares those behaviors and actions with millennials that make senior leaders take notice and can help advance their careers.

- **Show up looking the part.** One of the worst mistakes that young professionals make is not understanding the importance of looking like they belong. Whether you work in the buttoned-down world of Wall Street, the uniformed world of big box retailers (e.g., Target with their red tops and beige khakis), or the business casual culture that permeates today's typical workplace, it's important to dress in a manner that doesn't conflict with the culture. If the culture is conservative, shy away from loud or trendy clothing or colors. Save your self-expressive wardrobe for after hours. In addition to clothing, be mindful of your accessories as well. In the artsy and creative world of advertising, marketing, or social media, it may be acceptable to wear jewelry that grabs attention. But those same bulky bracelets, big hoop earrings, and shiny bling-bling rings and necklaces may be

---

[106] Robert Deitz, "Congratulations You Just Got Hired: Don't Screw It Up," (Create Space Independent Publishing Platform, 2013).

viewed less favorably in a corporate headquarters, government agency, or warehouse floor. Likewise it may be wise to reconsider the nose rings, limit the exposure of tattoos, and go easy with the exotic nail care designs. The intent is not to take away your right to be an individual but rather to avoid drawing unnecessary, unwanted, and unflattering attention to yourself.

- **Show up with innovative ideas.** Although they may never admit it publically, many baby boomers and Gen Xers struggle when it comes to driving innovation and looking for new ways to solve problems. This is particularly true when it comes to leveraging the use of technology. For millennials this provides a unique opportunity to add value from day one. If you show up to meetings with ideas and suggestions on how to streamline processes, introduce new products and services, or outperform a competitor, you will get the attention of those in leadership. Being able to demonstrate thought leadership and create value can be your ticket to that next promotion, company project, or special recognition.

- **Show up ready to play.** One of the biggest knocks against young professionals is that we lack the motivation to roll up our sleeves and get the job done. Part of this perception (I say "myth") is because of how others interpret our chill attitudes. It's not that we aren't concerned or appreciate starting early or staying late; it's just that we would rather work smart than work hard. Additionally as children who grew up multitasking, we can listen to our iPod and get the job done at the same time. But many of our older peers view such behavior negatively. My father was livid when a college intern he hired while serving as president of U.S. Operations at Pitney Bowes would perform her work with her earbuds in, listening to Jay-Z. In his way of thinking, there was no way she could have the attention to detail required to perform the task with rap music blasting in her ear. While it may be true that we have mastered how to multitask effectively, in reality, today men and women who think like my father lead the business world. They grew up with a formula for success that said, "Show up early, stay late, and work hard." Waxing nostalgic to his days of playing basketball, my dad would always say, "If practice starts at six AM, you don't show up at six AM. You are on the court, ready to play at six AM."

- **Show up with your eyes open.** One of the hardest lessons I had to learn as a young professional was, to some degree, "It's a jungle out there." In the work world, people are all competing to some degree. As such, not everyone is your friend, not everyone is a team player, and not everyone is happy to see you. While I abhor the idea of playing politics, it would be naïve not to be aware of the political landscape. Like the lion watching the cute little gazelle, if you show up unaware or unconcerned regarding your surroundings, you will be eaten alive. However, showing up with your eyes open doesn't mean living in paranoia. Rather it means understanding that everything about you sends a message and you want to be aware of the messages you are sending.
    o **Technology and Social Media:** Be careful not only of what you post to social media away from the job, but be aware of how you use your company-provided technology. It can be embarrassing (and possibly career-ending) if your digital footprint reveals excessive amounts of time on shopping sites, social sites, or, worse yet, adult content sites.
    o **Professional Distance:** While it is important to be friendly, cordial, and a team player, it's imperative not to become too open and comfortable about your personal life. Likewise it's vital to understand the organization's culture and hierarchy. Your boss is not your BFF. Joking around with your peers may be fine, but the same chummy behavior may not be well received from your vice president. Another no-no on my father's list is DWYW, or dating where you work. In full transparency I'm not 100 percent in agreement on this one. I believe it is possible to meet someone at work, start a friendship, and, if it grows into a relationship, professionally behave in the workplace. My father, on the other hand, believes this is a problem waiting to happen. His thoughts are, given the emotional nature of relationships, it

is virtually impossible for these emotions to not manifest in the workplace. Furthermore, when (and I say if) the relationship ends, it can create an uncomfortable situation for everyone involved.

- o **The Importance of Attitude:** Showing up with the right attitude is also important. No one likes working with a Debbie Downer or someone who is always negative. This is not to suggest that everyone should be a Pollyanna, but whenever possible, try to maintain a "glass is half full" perspective and focus more on the solution than the problem. Another corny but insightful saying my father has is, "I'll give you ten points for identifying the problem, but I'll give you ninety points for coming up with a solution."

- **Show up current and relevant.** We live in an ever-changing world. We get news around the clock, social media updates constantly, and new information delivered to our fingertips every minute of the day. It can be overwhelming and create an information overload. However, in the workplace, it is essential that young professionals "stay current to remain relevant," as Dad says. If information and ideas are the new currency of the twenty-first century, young professionals need to be rich and well-informed. Yes, we have our degrees, but learning doesn't end in the classroom. It begins when you leave the classroom. If I were to ask you, "Where do you get your information from on a daily basis?" What would your answer be? If I wanted the list of business books or periodicals you've read in the past three months, what would your list look like? If I were to open up your organization's annual report, would you be able to have a meaningful conversation about your company's goals, strategies, and performance? If we are to be taken seriously and add value, we need to be as deliberate in updating our knowledge base as we are in updating our social media status.

More Rules for Connecting Like a Rock Star

After graduating with a master of social work degree from the University of Southern California, Jodi Brockington found her niche in the nonprofit sector. While working with a South Central-based youth agency, she served as a key player in drafting a grant proposal that garnered $750,000. Shortly after the sponsorship came through, the organization's senior leaders shuffled in new employees who walked in the door, earning double what Brockington was offered in her role.

The woman who she thought would be her advocate—the woman who was her mentor and the woman who was her boss—put her tail between her legs. After that moment Brockington realized she had more to offer herself and there was a greater work for her to do.

That tough lesson helped turn her into a master connector, partnering with powerhouse organizations such as Count Me In, Girls Inc., and the National Urban League to empower women to connect and lead with confidence.

She abides by six simple networking rules that you too can use to become a rock star connector.

- **Put on your happy face.** It turns out the secret to succeeding in your career, getting better service, or even scoring a few extra dates is no surprise at all. Smiling can attract more than admiring looks. Sincere smiles send off positive vibes that tell people you're a confident and friendly person worth getting to know. When you're meeting people and trying to get noticed, this is crucial. People don't want the Debbie Downers; they want the Happy Harrietts to brighten their day.
- **If you're a giver, recognize that the getting will come later.** The ultimate quality of being an extraordinary connector is also being an excellent giver. It's not about "What can I do for me?" Rather it's "What can I do for you?"
- **Take stock of your strengths and ways you can put those assets to use.** In certain situations, you may find that what you're good at doesn't necessarily translate to using a skill. Your gift might just consist of being helpful or nice. Sometimes a single act of

kindness has more power to open doors to once-in-a-lifetime opportunities than you could ever imagine.
- **Listen with a focus.** The beauty of being a brilliant listener means you can become a better problem solver. Think about it. When you take the time to really hear what a person has to say, you'll find he or she is only searching for solutions. And if you pay close attention, you could be the answer he or she is counting on.
- **Bond outside of business.** Answer true or false. Most deals are made outside of the boardroom. If you answered true, you're correct. Numerous partnerships are nurtured through intimate exchanges at informal affairs. Many professionals hurt themselves by not going on the golf trips because they don't play golf. That's just silly. In case you didn't know, it's not about the game. It's about the time with those influencers.
- **Don't forget the follow-up.** This final rule makes all the others work together. You could be really great at making connections, but if you don't leverage the relationship, it was almost pointless to have a conversation in the first place.

Remember: you want to be the connector. Be authentic. Be consistent. Be graceful.[107]

The Baby Boomer's Reaction: It's Not Your Father's Workplace

For many the issue regarding the career advancement expectations of millennials is the crux of the matter. Baby boomers feel that millennials want it all and they want it now. Not only that, they want it where they want it, when they want it, and how they want it! On the other hand, millennials refuse to adhere to antiquated models of career advancement, management style, or work hour expectations. The organizations that will be most successful in today's environment are those that can best leverage the energy, intelligence, and innovation of their millennial workforce with the wisdom and experience of their more seasoned workers.

---

[107] "Jodi Brockington Keynote," Black Enterprise Golf and Tennis Challenge, August 2014.

Advice to Millennials

- Understand that the best leaders have touched several bases or held a variety of experiences that give them a unique perspective. While it is possible to be successful as a millennial leader, understand that your effectiveness will increase over time as you learn from your various experiences.
- Be open to relocation. Those willing to relocate for new roles will have more opportunities for advancement.
- Be sensitive to older workers who might feel awkward reporting to someone young enough to be their sons or daughters. It doesn't mean you don't lead or manage performance. Just be aware of how others have to learn to appreciate working for you.
- While it doesn't have to take ten years, be patient and realistic regarding your career advancement expectations. Rome wasn't built in a day.

Advice to Boomers

- Check your ego at the door. While these millennials may be young and somewhat naïve, they are the future.
- Look for opportunities to serve as mentors to them and share your knowledge of the organization, your wisdom, and your experiences.

Chapter 7

Stir Up Start-up Success

Tips for Turning Your Passion into Profits

From start-ups to side hustles, millennials are stirring up a movement to become self-made. Yes, the so-called lazy generation is empowered to become entrepreneurs, and research proves we are actually finding some success at it. A 2014 Deloitte millennial leadership study showed that, more than other generations, millennials are eager to become self-employed at a younger age and are willing to take major career risks to make it happen. A surprising 70 percent of global millennials want to launch their own companies.[108]

---

[108] Dan Schawbel, "Alexandra Levit: How Millennials Will Shake Things Up at Work," *Forbes*, February 28, 2014, http://www.forbes.com/sites/danschawbel/2014/02/28/alexandra-levit-how-millennial-entrepreneurs-will-shake-things-up-at-work.

Lisa Curtis, founder of Kuli Kuli, a food start-up that aims to improve global nutrition, says that nearly one in five millennials are preparing to leave their jobs to launch their own business.[109] Given the current state of the economy, it's quite shocking that Gen Y is so eager to step out into such dangerous territory. It's no secret that the majority of start-ups fail before they are given a fair chance to get off the ground. According to Curtis, 99 percent of start-ups that seek venture capital are rejected. And of the lucky 1 percent who are fortunate enough to receive financing, only 25 percent are able to provide a return on investment.

What does it mean for business and society when

- our young people are more likely to run a Kickstarter campaign than run for political office
- the epitome of success isn't a steady job at a well-known company but building an app that's like Facebook for a certain niche group
- the ownership of an Etsy store or organic food truck are viable career paths?[110]

Small business expert Donna Fenn, author of *Upstarts!*, foresees millennials being the most seasoned, most experienced entrepreneurial leaders in history. In her book, which chronicles the journeys of 150 Gen Y business owners, Fenn found that aspiring millennial moguls are overwhelmingly collaborative, tech-savvy, and agile. They're also socially conscious. They focus on work-life balance, and they strive to create high performing, but fun workplaces.

She attributes this to millennials being the first generation to grow up with entrepreneurial role models like Steve Jobs, Bill Gates, Anita Roddick, Richard Branson, and, later, Sergey Brin and Larry Page, Steve Chen and Chad Hurley, Mark Zuckerberg, Kevin Rose, and so forth. Just as Gen Yers have no memory of life without computers and the Internet, they also have no memory of a time when successful entrepreneurs were not imbued with rock star status. And they've never

---

[109] Lisa Curtis, "The Millennial Startup Revolution," *Forbes Woman*, November 18, 2013, http://www.forbes.com/sites/85broads/2013/11/18/the-millennial-startup-revolution.

[110] Ibid.

had the expectation of lifetime employment in corporate America. So they approach entrepreneurship very much from a lifestyle perspective. They want to live the entrepreneurial life, and for many of them, that will mean starting multiple companies.[111]

Top Factors Fueling Aspiring Millennial Moguls

Steve Jobs once said, "The ones who are crazy enough to think that they can change the world, are the ones who do."[112]

- **Being an entrepreneur has become a mind-set critical to career success.** Entrepreneurship is now accessible to everyone regardless of age or occupation. You don't need to own a business to be an entrepreneur, but you do need the entrepreneurial mind-set to be successful in business. Millennials believe being self-made carries certain leadership characteristics required for success, including being a self-starter, risk-taker, visionary, and someone who spots opportunity.[113]
- **Freelancers enjoy more freedom.** A 2013 oDesk and Millennial Branding study of 3,193 freelancers around the world, including nearly 2,000 millennials, revealed that the primary driving force behind young professionals following independent careers is the flexibility and freedom that being your own boss affords the freedom to
    o choose their work environment (92 percent)
    o set their own schedules (87 percent)
    o work on their personal passions (69 percent)

---

[111] Scott Gerber, "The Upstarts Are Coming," *Entrepreneur*, December 20, 2009, http://www.entrepreneur.com/article/204432.

[112] Carmine Gallo, "10 Powerful Quotes from the Steve Jobs Movie and What They Teach Us about Leadership," *Forbes*, August 16, 2013, http://www.forbes.com/sites/carminegallo/2013/08/16/10-powerful-quotes-from-the-steve-jobs-movie-and-what-they-teach-us-about-leadership.

[113] Shoshana Deutschkron and Dan Schawbel, "Groundbreaking Survey Reveals the Rise of Freedom Seeking Freelancers and Redefinition of Entrepreneurship," oDesk, May 14, 2013, https://www.odesk.com/info/about/press/releases/groundbreaking-survey-reveals-rise-freedom-seeking-freelancers-and-redefinition-entrepreneurship.

- travel while working (64 percent)
- **They make the most out of an unemployed situation.** It doesn't take a government shutdown to tell you how incredibly fragile our economy still is. According to *Time*, 64 percent of young Americans ages sixteen to twenty-four who are enrolled in school do not have a full-time job, which is 10 percent less than in 2007. We're nowhere near the unemployment of young Spaniards (56 percent) or Greek youth (58 percent), but the unappetizing prospect of remaining unemployed or working a low-wage internship has inspired many of us to crown ourselves as CEO.[114]
- **They distrust corporate leadership.** Wall Street crashed our economy, polarized politicians shut down our government, and the news is rife with reports of corruption at the top (for example, Mark Sanford, Bob Filner, and Kwane Kilpatrick). No wonder less than half of Americans trust the government, and less than that place faith in Wall Street. Once we can no longer rely on our leaders to solve our problems for us, many of us look within and build our own solutions for a diverse array of problems such as climate change (Mosaic), childhood obesity (Revolution Foods), and access to sanitation (Who Gives a Crap).[115]

Common Mistakes That Sabotage Our Start-up Success

Considering the odds stacked against start-ups, it is quite surprising that Gen Y is willing to gamble as green entrepreneurs. After spending the last decade running her own business consulting for companies and corporations, Dana Brownlee, president of Atlanta-based training firm Professionalism Matters, says newbie entrepreneurs make seven "alarmingly consistent" common mistakes.[116]

---

[114] Lisa Curtis, "The Millennial Startup Revolution," *Forbes Woman*, November 18, 2013, http://www.forbes.com/sites/85broads/2013/11/18/the-millennial-startup-revolution.

[115] Ibid.

[116] Dana Brownlee, "7 Sins of Newbie Entrepreneurs," *Entrepreneur*, March 7, 2014, http://www.entrepreneur.com/article/232021.

- **Mistake No. 1: Not setting aside enough cash reserves to support yourself.** Brownlee believes that one of the reasons why so many small businesses fail within the first few years is not because the business model isn't viable or the entrepreneur isn't good enough to make the business work. Most entrepreneurs simply run out of money to support the business and/or themselves before the business is profitable enough to sustain itself.
- **Mistake No. 2: Using assumptions that are overly optimistic during planning.** So many newbie entrepreneurs fall into this trap. They have a great idea and convinced their friends and family that it's a no-brainer. They jump into the fray, only to realize there were a few not-so-little details that they failed to consider or some areas where their assumptions were overly optimistic. And before they know it, that no-brainer business is hanging by a thread.
- **Mistake No. 3: Not properly evaluating your business model.** Not everyone incorporates a business model into his or her planning. It's so easy to get really lathered up around the concept of your business, but it's quite another thing to put pen to paper to help you objectively evaluate your overall business model and its profit potential. The simple truth is that having a great idea is just a start. It doesn't necessarily translate into a profitable model.
- **Mistake No. 4: Trying to do everything yourself to save money.** If you try to do everything yourself, not only will you run yourself into the ground, your business will suffer because you don't bring sufficient expertise in every area. Your time is money. Think about where you must personally invest your energies. Should you be developing and refining your content, products, and services; cultivating relationships with key clients and stakeholders; and developing credibility within your industry? No one can do this for you. That said, others could develop your website, handle your public relations, develop templates for your newsletters, make trips to printers

- **Mistake No. 5: Not being willing to work like a dog during the early days.** Brownlee says she is amazed how often she runs into people who've recently launched their businesses but seem shocked that they're not making six figures while working a twenty-five-hour workweek. They seem to have this glamorous view of entrepreneurship where they get to start at the top and skip all the hard work. The simple truth is, if you want to make it, most start-up businesses have to hustle early on. This might mean working another job while you're starting your business, volunteering, or doing some work for free to gain experience and exposure. It also may mean working nights and weekends.
- **Mistake No. 6: Pricing your product or services too low or high.** In her business Brownlee often responds to request for proposals. Years ago she'd been submitting proposal responses annually to a large governmental agency. After about four years of consistent rejections, she got a tip from a colleague that her pricing was too low to be considered seriously. That year she doubled her pricing on the same classes and was selected for the first time.
- **Mistake No. 7: Not having a growth strategy.** We all know of a restaurant that was great when it first opened but went downhill after expanding the food or service. They then developed a bad reputation and eventually closed. Don't be that business.

While most small businesses think the goal is to win as much business as they can, this isn't necessarily true. Sometimes you can attract too much business and then have a completely different challenge that could threaten the long-term viability of the business completely.

Boss Moves Tips from Dana Brownlee

1. Before jumping into the start-up world, really evaluate your current lifestyle and realize you will most likely give up a huge chunk, if not all, your free time.
2. Proactively set up a special fund intended to support yourself during the business start-up phase. Be conscious of what you put into this fund, as you may want to strive for an amount that can fully support you for a year or two to relieve pressure as you ramp up.
3. Find three to five completely objective people (not friends or family) and specifically ask them to play devil's advocate to you to help identify vulnerabilities and then take steps to mitigate those.
4. Consider SCORE or a small business development center to evaluate the business model and offer expert advice. Their perspective could identify a more viable structure that makes better business sense than what you've already established.
5. Identify what you can outsource and what you can manage. A good rule of thumb is, if it's not part of the core competency of your specific business, you have little expertise in the area, it's time-consuming, and many suppliers can provide the service at a reasonable cost, consider outsourcing.
6. Don't under- or overvalue your business. Do your research to see what others are charging. It's much smarter to offer value pricing initially, prove your value, and then raise prices over time. In many cases, not only will asking clients for their budget give you an idea of what to charge, it could minimize the risk of severely under- or overpricing your product or services. You may also consider providing different pricing options to increase the likelihood that you're offering something within your client's price range.

Think about how you want to grow and develop a high-level growth strategy fairly early on, even if it changes as time progresses.[117]

A Millennial Mogul Making It Happen

It would have been so easy to feature Facebook founder and CEO Mark Zuckerburg as the glue that holds this conversation on millennial entrepreneurship together. After all, Facebook is a social media force, and he is the first millennial CEO. There's no question that his trailblazing story speaks to the genius of the millennial mind like Steve Jobs did for baby boomers. But in truth we need to read stories about people grinding and hustling their hearts out to get their businesses off the ground, who, just like the Nike slogan, get up every day and do it, whether or not the revenue is pouring in, the resources are available, or the reality that their dream will take flight is easy.

They say the best way to find your own path is to get lost on your present one. No one is a better example of that than Necole Kane. Today the blogger/entrepreneur sits in the driver's seat of a burgeoning empire that includes the Urban Entertainment blog, NecoleBitchie.com; its Lifestyle offspring, XONecole; the web channel, BitchieTV; and a forthcoming apparel line, BC Society. But what a difference three years can make.

Though Necole's Bitchie online persona made its debut onto the blogging scene in 2008, the motivation behind building her brand really began when she was a child growing up in a small town on the eastern shore of Maryland, spending her free time daydreaming, creating movies in her mind, and writing books that were never finished. In college she majored in television and film with a hope of becoming the next Mara Brock Akil or female John Singleton.

Shortly after Necole's father passed away, and her mother followed two years later. She felt lost and uninspired and came down with a terrible case of writer's block. Looking for a fresh start she moved to Detroit and began an internship with a radio station as a producer, her first taste of working in entertainment. Six months later she was hired as the assistant marketing director/promotions coordinator, where she was

---

[117] Ibid.

introduced to marketing and brand strategizing and the importance of building a branding platform. After music executive Lyor Cohen visited the radio station and gave a presentation on his artists at Warner Music Group, a light bulb came on for Necole. She would work for a record label.

The young entrepreneur hopeful quit her job, moved to New York City, and interviewed with numerous record labels and management companies, but her lack of experience kept her from nabbing the job of her dreams. By the summer of 2007, a frustrated Necole decided she would never send out another résumé, and she never did. Unfortunately, however, by the beginning of 2008, Necole found herself broke and forced to move in with her aunt.

Necole recalls, "I was in a situation where I felt like I had lost everything while trying to take risks. My career. Money. My parents. I was devastated." She was back in the small town where she was raised where the two most viable employers were Walmart and a pickle plant. And Necole was sure that her entertainment industry dreams were over. "I'm sitting in the guest room at my aunt's house thinking to myself, I've failed. I've truly failed. What are people going to say about me?"[118]

After getting her hands on the popular self-help book, *The Secret*, Necole decided she had no time for self-pity. She needed a plan, so she concluded, "There is a lack of jobs in the industry, so I'm going to create my own."[119] Seeing a lack of coverage in urban entertainment, Necole Bitchie was born as she began reporting on the world of celebrity entertainment and new music while blogging some of her personal experiences as well.

"I wanted to connect with my readers on a level that I hadn't seen on other urban sites that I had frequented. That helped me stand out."[120] Though her following on her website grew quickly, a new challenge emerged. Unable to understand why Necole spent the majority of her time on the Internet versus looking for employment, her aunt kicked

---

[118] "About," NecoleBitchie.com, accessed September 3, 2014, http://iamnecole.com/about.

[119] Ibid.

[120] Ibid.

her out, leading her to Atlanta, completely alone again, to figure out how to make it work.

"I was hurt because the only thing I had was a roof over my head, and you go and take that too. That was the worst thing that I thought could happen to me at that time, but now, I see that it was truly a blessing. It gave me only one option, and that was to make it."[121]

Within a year, NecoleBitchie.com became one of the leading and fastest-growing urban gossip sites on the Internet, attracting readers, advertisers, and such esteemed outlets as the Huffington Post, CNN, *Boston Globe*, Global Grind, VIBE, and BET. The very industry that had once rejected her now courted her.

Now her accolades include Black Enterprise's Black Blogger of the Month, Soul Train Music Award for Best Soul Site, the Black Weblog Awards Best Gossip Blog and Blogger of the Year honors, and *Ebony*'s Power 100. She was the first blogger to appear on BET's *106th and Park*, all while being featured in *Sister 2 Sister, Essence, J'Adore, Rolling Out*, Huffington Post, *Tom Joyner Morning Show, The Breakfast Club Morning Show*, and more.[122]

Not only is Necole on her way to building a media empire that will include a production house, clothing and beauty line, and social applications, she is creating a nonprofit that will mentor and provide financial support to further the education of children who have lost their parents prematurely.

Necole exemplifies what it means to gain control of one's self through self-determination, self-motivation, self-reliance, and self-promotion. More important than any of her accomplishments, however, is Necole's focus on making sure people, especially young girls, find inspiration in her story. This desire led her to create IAMNECOLE.com. She says,

> I hope I am able to connect with my readers more on a personal level and provide inspiration. I want to motivate others to take risks and go hard for what they want out of life. I especially want girls to know that you should never let anyone get away with telling you that

---

[121] Ibid.

[122] Ibid.

you aren't worth it, or you won't make it. If you truly believe in yourself, it doesn't matter what people think because ultimately as long as you have a dream and a plan of action, no one can stop you.[123]

The Baby Boomer's Reaction: Do Your Thing!

Of all the things I admire about millennials, it's their creativity and entrepreneurial spirit. Unlike my generation, which viewed success as landing a great job with a great company, many millennials embrace the vision of starting their own companies. In some ways, I believe many baby boomers secretly envy our millennial cohorts, wishing we had had the courage and willingness to become entrepreneurs. Many of us have worked thirty-plus years, only to find that the satisfaction of our 401(k) plans can't make up for the "what might have been" feelings buried deep inside.

Advice to Millennials

- Do your homework before launching out on your own. Understand the size of the market, competition, capital required, and realistic demand for your product or service.
- Create a business plan complete with goals, objectives, timelines, anticipated start-up costs, risks, and revenue potential.
- Seek out those who are already in the business to shorten your learning curve.

Advice to Boomers

- It's never too late. What better time than now to leverage your years of experience and know-how and work for yourself?

---

[123] Ibid.

Chapter 8

If I Knew Then What I Know Now

A Conversation with My Twentysomething Self

For the first seven chapters of this book, my daughter Alana framed the dialogue of this book. Given that the primary audience is her peer group, it made sense that she take the lead in speaking to them. As a card-carrying AARP member for many years now, so many of the ideas, terminology, and logic of the millennial world is foreign to me. I pay someone to manage my social media. I don't tweet, send instant messages, or use the cloud. I'm still using email. I send text messages only when my kids don't answer my call. And yes, I still check voice mail.

However, I was honored when my daughter asked me to use the last chapter to share my philosophies on career management and advancement. She got the idea of me sharing my thoughts after looking at a picture of me in my late twenties. Her initial reaction was shock, as she noticed I had hair back then. But once the humor subsided, she asked me a very intriguing question, "Dad, if you could go back in time and speak to your twentysomething self, what advice would you give yourself?"

It was a question I had given thought to over the years but never really sat down to give it meaningful consideration. As I pondered this question, my mind took twists and turns to all of the challenges I had to overcome, to the failures and successes of my career, to the highs and lows, and to the tears and the smiles.

The first thing I realized is something I didn't expect. In my life I learned more from my failures than I did from my successes. Make no mistake. My successes inspired me, but my failures and the lessons they provided paved the way for real growth, wisdom, and learning.

- My failed projects forced me to look for alternative answers.
- My failed presentations forced me to work on my communications skills.
- My failed relationships forced me to look in the mirror.
- My failure to get that raise, win that sale, or earn that promotion provided the inspiration and motivation to be the best I could be.

My second realization was another eye-opener. At the end of the day, it's all about the people. For years as a leader in the corporate world, the "end all, be all" was creating shareholder value. It was the idea that, as long as we focused on providing those institutions and individuals who owned our stock the highest possible return on their investment, all would be well with the world.

Now to be clear. I am still a big advocate for creating shareholder value. However, I've realized that the way to create that value is not by focusing solely on cutting costs or making quarterly goals. Rather it's taking care of the people who do the work, providing them with direction, treating them with respect and dignity, and helping them understand how they fit in the bigger picture, no matter how insignificant they might feel their role is. It's empowering them to be innovative and giving them a voice. By doing so, you'll create an engaged and energized workforce, people who take pride in their work, take great care of the customer, and ultimately drive revenue and profit. The best way to drive share price and create shareholder value is by taking care of the people.

My third and final observation, regardless of your industry, job function, or pay grade, will be one that every reader will have to address. Namely it's the ability to overcome adversity. I have found that the failures, disappointments, and discouragements determined my effectiveness. My ability to overcome adversity, setbacks, and disappointments proved most valuable. I have summed up my personal recipe for overcoming adversity in what I call the "Four Fs of Life," or faith, focus, fortitude, and fearlessness.

- **Faith:** It has been my experience that accomplishing anything in life requires faith first and foremost in yourself, your abilities, your potential, and your right to be where you are. As a spiritual person, I have also had to summon my faith in a higher power. When I have come to the end of myself and don't know what I can do, I have had to call on a power greater than I am to see me through. Some call it a higher power; others refer to it as the universe. Or in my case, He's the God Almighty. Regardless of the name, your faith will be tested on this journey, and you'll need to draw strength from someone bigger than you and I.
- **Focus**: One of the secrets of my success in both college and professionally has been my ability to stay focused on the goal, to keep my eye on the prize, regardless of the distractions and naysayers in my path. In a world that has allowed technology to create distractions 24-7 with social media, streaming video, unlimited talk and text, and automobiles enabled with Internet connectivity, it is easy to lose focus. Those who will be most effective will be the people who can maintain focus despite the distractions of twenty-first-century life.
- **Fortitude:** While there may be many definitions for the word "fortitude," the common denominator lies in the ability to courageously endure adversity. In your career, as in life, at times you will want to give up and give in. Perhaps your organization is going through a downsizing and you are impacted. Maybe you

find yourself in an organization that devalues you and causes you to lose confidence in yourself. Whatever the reason for the dilemma, hardship, or adversity, it's important to cultivate the mental and emotional stamina to endure. Life is about seasons, and just as spring follows winter, seasons do change. On this journey you must learn to press on in spite of.

- **Fearlessness:** There have been many seminal moments in my career where, had I chosen the safe option, it would have never prepared me for greater responsibility. I was never afraid to relocate to a part of the country I was unfamiliar with. I didn't fear taking over the underperforming division or department. I refused to be afraid of embracing new technology or a difficult boss or even joining an organization undergoing transformation. Too often we allow fear to rob of us experiences that would stretch us. We get into a comfort zone, staying with the familiar as opposed to taking on new experiences. During your journey resist the urge to play it safe when an opportunity faces you. You may discover that such opportunities serve to enhance your life, personally and professionally.

Enjoy the Journey

My last piece of advice is to embrace continuous learning and enjoy the journey. I have found that maintaining a sense of intellectual curiosity will help you be successful in any field. You will be able to add value in any organization and create and innovate beyond your wildest dreams. You will need to stay current to remain relevant. You can't rest on your laurels. You should never let your learning stop after you get that degree. On a daily basis, you should have a formalized process for receiving new information. Perhaps it's reviewing online versions of the *Wall Street Journal*, *Forbes*, or an industry-related website. Or it could be as simple as subscribing to the RSS feeds of your favorite news sites. Whatever your method, make continuous learning a priority.

Additionally, I strongly recommend that you learn to embrace the journey. Too often in the fast-paced, "climb the ladder and get there now" society, many of us focus on the destination, not the journey. In our desire to get to where we are going, we don't take time out to enjoy, engage, and embrace the experiences and lessons along the way. The destination is the end result, but the joy is in the journey. Take time to live in the moment, to enjoy the relationships, and to reflect on the lessons you've learned. Before you know it, thirty years will have passed, and you will have arrived at your destination. Enjoying the journey makes your arrival so much more fulfilling.

ABOUT THE AUTHOR

Alana Wyche is freelance writer and communications professional with more than six years of experience in the media industry. She previously served as a production manager at Black Enterprise-TV, where she oversaw the logistics for nationally syndicated television programming for the company's broadcast division.

Wyche received a bachelor of arts degree in communication, graduating cum laude from the University of Toledo. She is a member of Alpha Kappa Alpha Sorority, Inc.

***

Keith Wyche is a results-driven, no-nonsense executive with more than thirty years of experience in the corporate world at such companies such as AT&T, IBM, and Pitney-Bowes. Most recently as president, he turned around Cub Food and Acme Markets and led them to growth.

As a nationally recognized public speaker, Wyche has delivered keynotes to such organizations as Harvard University, Target, Kraft Foods, Dell, GE, and more. His first book, *Good Is Not Enough: And Other Unwritten Rules for Minority Professionals*, published by Portfolio, a division of Penguin Random House, was an Amazon best seller and nominated for the 2009 NAACP Image Award for Outstanding Literary Work. His 2013 book, *Corner Office Rules: The 10 Realities of Executive Life*, published by Kandelle Enterprises, opens the door to the often-hidden world of the C-suite.

ABOUT THE BOOK

The idea for this book was born when I first entered the workforce after college and realized that my father and I viewed the workplace very differently. I wanted to make an immediate impact at the company, while he insisted I fit in before attempting to stand out. I saw no harm in sharing my ideas and disagreeing with senior leadership. He suggested I respect authority. In my mind promotions should be based on merit, not tied to a time frame. In his view I needed to pay my dues and incur a few battle scars before even thinking of seeking a promotion.

Life at work became even more of a challenge when I realized that most of the leaders in the workplace shared my father's belief system. After careful reflection I realized that perhaps a generational divide was the true culprit. My father, who was born during the Eisenhower administration, was a baby boomer to his core. I, on the other hand, was born in 1984 and grew up with access to information, technology, and resources that my father never dreamed about as a child. Everything from the smartphone to the microwave, Internet, personal computer, social media, and so many other inventions and innovations allowed my generation to do things quicker, faster, and easier than ever before.

However, the challenge in today's workplace is, "How do you leverage the talents and strengths of everyone in order to make the organization better?" In today's über-competitive, information-driven global economy, the organizations who can best harness the collective power of all of its workforce will be the organizations to not only survive but thrive. But to accomplish such a feat requires cooperation, mutual respect, and a willingness to value our unique backgrounds, experiences, skills, and viewpoints.

This book serves to enhance your ability to succeed by exploring common myths and perceptions regarding millennials. You will see yourselves through the eyes of others in order to better understand and ultimately overcome these misperceptions. Additionally it will force you to look at yourself in the mirror to uncover some of your blind spots and opportunities for personal and professional growth.

Written by a millennial with editorial insights by her baby boomer father, the hope is that, after reading *Swag Is Not Enough*, the reader will have a better understanding of how our different ways of viewing the world can actually make the workplace and ultimately the world a better, more inclusive, and more innovative place.

www.ingramcontent.com/pod-product-compliance
Lightning Source LLC
Chambersburg PA
CBHW030817180526
45163CB00003B/1328